Comments on other *Amazing Stories* from readers & reviewers

"Tightly written volumes filled with lots of wit and humour about famous and infamous Canadians."
Eric Shackleton, *The Globe and Mail*

"The heightened sense of drama and intrigue, combined with a good dose of human interest is what sets Amazing Stories *apart."*
Pamela Klaffke, *Calgary Herald*

"This is popular history as it should be... For this price, buy two and give one to a friend."
Terry Cook, a reader from Ottawa, on **Rebel Women**

"Glasner creates the moment of the explosion itself in graphic detail...she builds detail upon gruesome detail to create a convincingly authentic picture."
Peggy McKinnon, *The Sunday Herald*, on **The Halifax Explosion**

"It was wonderful...I found I could not put it down. I was sorry when it was completed."
Dorothy F. from Manitoba on **Marie-Anne Lagimodière**

"Stories are rich in description, and bristle with a clever, stylish realness."
Mark Weber, *Central Alberta Advisor*, on **Ghost Town Stories II**

"A compelling read. Bertin...has selected only the most intriguing tales, which she narrates with a wealth of detail."
Joyce Glasner, *New Brunswick Reader*, on **Strange Events**

"The resulting book is one readers will want to share with all the women in their lives."
Lynn Martel, *Rocky Mountain Outlook*, on **Women Explorers**

AMAZING STORIES

GREAT STANLEY
CUP VICTORIES

GREAT STANLEY CUP VICTORIES

Glorious Moments in Hockey

HOCKEY

by Rich Mole

PUBLISHED BY ALTITUDE PUBLISHING CANADA LTD.
1500 Railway Avenue, Canmore, Alberta T1W 1P6
www.altitudepublishing.com
1-800-957-6888

Extreme care has been taken to ensure that all information presented in
this book is accurate and up to date. Neither the author nor the
publisher can be held responsible for any errors.

Publisher	Stephen Hutchings
Associate Publisher	Kara Turner
Series Editor	Jill Foran
Hockey Editor	Stephen Smith
Digital Photo Colouring	Scott Manktelow

We acknowledge the financial support of the Government
of Canada through the Book Publishing Industry Development
Program (BPIDP) for our publishing activities.

Altitude GreenTree Program 🌲
Altitude Publishing will plant twice as many trees as were used
in the manufacturing of this product.

National Library of Canada Cataloguing in Publication Data

Mole, Rich, 1946-
Great Stanley Cup victories / Rich Mole.

(Amazing stories)
Includes bibliographical references.
ISBN 1-55153-797-4

1. Stanley Cup (Hockey) 2. National Hockey League--History.
3. Hockey--Canada--History. I. Title. II. Series: Amazing stories (Canmore,
Alta.)

GV847.7.M64 2004   796.962'648   C2004-902324-1

An application for the trademark for Amazing Stories™
has been made and the registered trademark is pending.

Printed and bound in Canada by Friesens
2 4 6 8 9 7 5 3 1

Cover: Wayne Gretzky holds the Stanley Cup after the 1984 finals.
(Credit: Bruce Bennett Studios)

To the fans — past, present, and future

Contents

Prologue

"I have, for some time, been thinking it would be a good thing if there was a challenge cup," Lord Stanley of Preston, Canada's sixth governor general, wrote. Pausing in his letter writing for just a moment, the country's pre-eminent hockey fan pondered his idea again. Yes, a challenge cup! Excitedly, Lord Stanley dipped his pen into the inkwell and bent over his sheet of official stationery once more. "…which should be held, from year to year to year, by the champion hockey club in the Dominion."

When Lord Stanley's aide read the letter out loud to the members of the Ottawa Athletic Association in March 1892, there were quick murmurs of agreement and appreciation. A challenge cup! Wonderful idea!

Soon after, during a trip to London, England, Lord Stanley took some time out from his round of official duties to do a little shopping. Walking about in a store, he spied a squat, silver bowl. Aha! Was this the cup? He picked it up, turning it this way and that, then smiled. It would do quite nicely. Taking his purchase to the counter, he had it wrapped for the journey back to Canada.

The very next year, the Stanley Cup's first competitors,

Montreal and Ottawa, skated out onto the ice wearing their high turtleneck sweaters and knitted wool caps. Though the small, squat cup cost no more than a few guineas (about $50 today), and though it would later be replaced by a 3-foot, 37-pound icon of excellence, its true worth was already being measured that very first year, by the sheer skill and determination it took to win it ...

Chapter 1
Ottawa Senators
Stanley Cup Victories: 1919–20,
1920–21, 1922–23, 1926–27

rank was listening for it. At this time of the
day, he was *always* listening for it: the
deep, rasping sound of the whistle — the
six o'clock train from Ottawa. The sound meant the latest
editions of the *Ottawa Journal* and *Ottawa Citizen* would
soon be waiting at the station. Inside those bundled newspapers, the latest feats of the Ottawa Senators would be waiting
for all to read. Waiting for *Frank* to read. When the sound of
the whistle floated across the town of Shawville, Frank was on
his feet and dashing out of the house. It was a kind of game
— get the news, know the news, before anyone else in town.
Sitting in a corner at the station, nine-year-old Frank
Finnigan devoured those sports pages and dreamed of

becoming a professional hockey player, of one day skating and scoring for his idolized teammates on the very best hockey team ever ...

Jump cut.

Like thousands of other Ottawa hockey fans, Tommy Gorman was ecstatic.

The 1919–20 season was over, and the Ottawa Senators were National Hockey League (NHL) champions. That meant the Senators would represent the new league in the Stanley Cup playoffs for the first time. And when those playoffs began, Gorman definitely wasn't going to be sitting in the stands high above the rink. After all, he was no ordinary fan.

As one of the Senators' two owners and the team's coach, Gorman would be exactly where you would expect him to be: down at ice-level, on his feet — pacing, shouting, and planning — as his boys in the striped jerseys squared off against the Western Hockey League's (WHL) Seattle Metropolitans. They were alternating two sets of rules — east and west — but so what? The Ottawa Senators had been the team to beat since they were called the Silver Seven, and had won three Stanley Cups back-to-back, long before Gorman and other team-owners had even hatched the NHL plot.

Freeze frame.

The WHL? What was *that*? The Seattle Metropolitans? The Silver Seven? An owner who was also the coach? The NHL *plot*? What's going on here?

It was a different world in 1920, and, in many ways,

hockey was a different game.

The game itself wasn't especially new. The first officially documented contest had been played — with a wooden puck — some 42 years earlier in Montreal. However, several important things *were* new, including the National Hockey League itself.

The National Hockey Association (NHA) had been Eastern Canada's dominant hockey institution since 1910. It was not a happy organization. The source of the discontent was irascible club-owner Eddie Livingstone. Livingstone's nay-saying and second-guessing — plus the fact that the man owned both Toronto teams — had other owners gritting their teeth. Livingstone had to go. How to do it? Simple: reorganize. Start anew.

Gorman and all the other team owners (except Livingstone) met in Montreal's Windsor Hotel to plan a replacement for the NHA. They called their new organization the National Hockey League. Working without Livingstone would be a relief. When the 1917–18 hockey season began, the NHA was history — and so was Livingstone.

"He was always arguing about everything," Gorman complained to Montreal sportswriter Elmer Ferguson after that initial strategy meeting. "Without him, we can get down to the business of making money."

When that inaugural 22-game NHL season began in December, four teams took to the ice: a new Toronto club called the Arenas, the Montreal Canadiens, a second

Montreal team called the Wanderers, and the Ottawa Senators. At that time, none of the team owners, least of all Tommy Gorman, could have foreseen that their new league was soon destined to take hockey to unimaginable heights of popularity and profit. Nor could Tommy ever have guessed that the success of the league he helped establish would ultimately doom the team that he would nurture and lead to such enduring distinction.

The First Dynasty
"Best Hockey Team In the World, 1917–27," the Senators' team photo boasted. By 1927, nobody could argue with the team's scintillating statistics. In less than ten incredible years, the Senators would lead the league an unparalleled seven times, win four Stanley Cups (when no other NHL team had won more than one), and become the first team to win back-to-back Cup victories. The Senators would also showcase trailblazing players who would win both the Hart (MVP) and Lady Byng (Sportsman) trophies for the first time, win the Art Ross Trophy for scoring excellence six times, set the record for scoring in consecutive games (16 straight), and be enshrined in the Hockey Hall of Fame.

This wasn't the usual complement of four or five Hall of Famers from a particular era of a team's history. Instead, a jaw-dropping, eye-widening total of 15 legendary Senator stars would be inducted into the Hall. What is even more astonishing is that this number represented almost half the team's complete decade-spanning roster of just 36 players! Professional hockey had never seen anything like this squad, and it would be decades before fans would again marvel at such a powerhouse team.

But on the warm, spring day of March 21, 1920, Tommy Gorman — *Ottawa Citizen* sports editor, hockey team owner, manager, and coach — wasn't thinking that far into the future. That day, he was focused completely on the next 24 hours. The Seattle Metropolitans had just stepped off the train to the cheering welcome of 2000 Ottawa hockey fans. The Senators would meet the western team on the ice of Laurier Street Arena the very next day. It was Stanley Cup time, again!

Different Time, Different League.

In the 1920s, Cup contests were fought in Vancouver, Edmonton, and Victoria, as well as Toronto, Montreal, Ottawa, New York, and Boston. Early in the decade, it was an east-west rivalry that embraced three separate leagues: the Pacific Coast Hockey Association, the Western Hockey League, and the NHL. To complicate matters even further, eastern and western teams played with different strengths. Eastern teams played with six on a side. The west still favoured the old-fashioned seven-man team, which included a "rover" position. Each league had its own rules. Even then, intense rivalries developed.

When Tommy Gorman learned that the first 1920 Cup

game was a sell-out, he was delighted, but not surprised. In many ways, the nation's capital was really a "town." Ottawa's intimate size made it easy to think of its heroes as hometown boys. As well, most of the Senators actually lived in Ottawa and were well known by sight. Some had grown up in the capital. Many others lived just a few kilometres away, in nearby Shawville, Pembroke, and Buckingham. That made Senator hockey feel like a family affair.

Strengthening the ties that bind was the feeling of isolation shared by most communities before high-speed freeways, air travel, and even radio came to be. The only way fans could get the latest on the "big game" a few dozen kilometres away was to hang around the telegraph office. At rinkside, Canadian Pacific Railway (CPR) and Great Northwestern telegraphers hunched down over their key, and, with the prompting of nearby sports reporters, clicked out the play-by-play in Morse code.

"Play now very fast and furious," one turn-of-the-century telegrapher tapped out.

"Excitement all over the rink. The puck is now travelling faster than I can handle the telegraph key ..."

Back home, the receiving telegrapher would decipher the dit-dit-dits into English and post the news on a community bulletin board.

The First League Superstars
On the first night of the 1919–20 five-game Cup series, 7500

noisy Ottawa fans made their way to seats that cost as much as $2.20 each, desperate to see their local favourites beat the Americans. As the players skated onto the ice, the fans let loose. There was Cy Denneny! Denneny had played first in the 1916–17 season, and had quickly established his reputation as a top scoring player. By stepping repeatedly on his stick, he'd fashioned himself a curved blade. Was that the secret that won him the Art Ross Trophy that season and another five times in the decade?

The fans yelled their encouragement to debonair Jack Darragh, the mercurial forward who was to spend his entire 13-year career with the Senators. There were also special shouts of recognition for Harry (Punch) Broadbent, whose record for goals in consecutive games would stand for generations. He would play for the Senators in two future Stanley Cup finals.

Fans roared their support for two other "hometown boys" who skated out into view. It was a warm, welcoming noise both players would hear for many seasons to come. Center Frank Nighbor — the Flying Dutchman — smiled as he looked up at the packed stands. This was not only the start of the Senators' dynasty, it was the start of Nighbor's dynasty, too. The "poke-checking wizard" would hammer his opponents with unerring speed and toughness, and, for all of that, earn the league's new Lady Byng Memorial Trophy for "the Best Type of Sportsmanship" (and he would do it again and again). Skating out with Nighbor was Clint Benedict. All was well with suave Benedict in the crease. It had been a great year for the goalie, setting the league record of five shutouts in the 24-game season. (It was Benedict — not Jacques Plante — who became the first goaltender to strap on a mask, a crude leather affair meant to protect a broken nose.)

The puck came down on the first face-off …

A Dynasty Begins

Late in the third period, the Seattle squad was ahead 2-1. Then came the moment the fans had been waiting for: Frank Nighbor took charge. With 10 minutes remaining, he stole the puck at center ice and raced past two Metropolitan defenders to score the tying goal. Six minutes later, Darragh slipped one past the Seattle goalie. For a second the crowd sat in stunned silence. Then all hell broke loose. It was a sight-and-sound riot of throat-searing cheers, flying hats, fluttering pennants, and whirling coats. The Senators had taken the first game 3-2.

Game two was a "soaker." The early March temperature sat around 5 degrees Celsius, and players from both teams were drenched from top to toe as the Senators splashed their way to a 3-0 shutout. The Seattle squad took its revenge in game three, beating the Senators 3-1, and sending both Nighbor and Darragh to the bench before the end of the game, too exhausted to play any further.

There would be no more "bathing suit" hockey. The fourth game was moved —much to the chagrin of Ottawa fans — to Toronto's Mutual Street Arena and that miracle of the modern sports world: artificial ice. But the cold, hard surface failed to help the Senators, and Seattle took the game 5-2.

Back in the dressing room, disgusted at the loss, Jack Darragh threw down his skates and announced that he'd had enough hockey for the winter, thank you very much.

Before anyone could stop him, the unpredictable player was on a train back to Ottawa and his chickens (he was raising Rhode Island Reds). He was talked onto the train again in time to dress for the fifth and deciding game two days later in Toronto. As it turned out, Darragh was destined to become its star.

The game was tied 1-1 until early in the third period. Darragh slipped through the

Metropolitans' defence and, in the words of a newspaper report, "scored the goal that cracked the hearts of the Seattle players." One was not enough. He scored two of the additional four Senator goals in the period for the hat trick, and the Senators took the game — and the Cup — on a 6-1 victory. Meanwhile, each player collected a victory bonus of $390.97 — a sum that even Darragh was quick to agree wasn't exactly chicken feed.

The Dynasty Gathers Momentum
At the end of the next season, it was the league-leading Senators' turn to pack its bags. The 1920–21 team was bound for British Columbia and their second NHL Cup Series in a row, facing the Pacific Coast League champions, the

Vancouver Millionaires. When the conductor hollered "all aboard," Punch Broadbent didn't climb the steps of the CPR Pullman alone. That afternoon, he had married Leda Fitzsimmons. Punch brought his new bride along for the ride, and the couple turned the team's trip into their honeymoon.

Many wondered if Jack Darragh would make the trip. He wanted to, but his new employer, the Ottawa Dairy, was less enthusiastic. It took the mayor's intervention to get Darragh the time off from work. In an era of slow train travel, that time was not inconsiderable: the team left on March 16 and would not return for almost three weeks.

When the Senators arrived on the coast, they found a city, as the *Vancouver Sun* phrased it, "seized by hockey fever." Inside the rink, the fever escalated as over 10,000 delirious fans watched their team take the first game 3-1. It wasn't the unfamiliar seven-man western rule that flummoxed the Senators. It was the tactics of the Millionaires' goalie, Hugh Lehman. Lehman caught the Ottawa team off guard repeatedly when he "shot the puck like lightning speed to awaiting forwards at center ice." Teams were not allowed to make forward passes in their defensive zone, in the attacking zone, or across blue lines. The one exception was the goaltender, who was allowed to pass as far as the blue line. Smelling blood, BC fans scooped up every available ticket for the second game in just two hours.

Scoring twice in less than three minutes of game two, the Millionaires appeared ready to demolish the Senators again. Ottawa fought back, tying the game up 3-3 at the end of the second period. Punch Broadbent hadn't travelled across Canada to lose two in a row! Late in the third period, the newlywed placed the deciding goal for a 4-3 win. The momentum continued to build and the Senators took the next game, 3-2. Vancouver battled back to win game four with the same score.

On April 4, it was standing room only as 12,000 fans jammed the arena to witness the final, decisive showdown. Outside, thousands of would-be spectators milled about waiting for word of what was going on inside. And there was plenty going on. The Vancouver Millionaires led the Senators 1-0 at the end of the first period. Jack Darragh put two in the net in the second period, and the Senators' famous defence clamped down hard, hoping to ride out the scoring advantage.

With two minutes remaining, it was all too much for Vancouver's Lloyd Cook.

The exasperated, exhausted defenceman let fly, punching Senator captain Eddie Gerard full in the face. Senator scrapper Sprague Cleghorn retaliated, giving Cook a one-two combination that sent him sprawling. Sticks clattered to the ice, fists were cocked, and the police were called in to pry the two teams apart. When play resumed, the Senators' defensive strength kept the 2-1 score unchanged: the Cup was theirs again. A week later, thousands lined the Ottawa parade route. Hundreds attended a lavish victory banquet at the Chateau Laurier.

Before the next season began, Tommy Gorman finally made the decision he'd been reluctant to make: he left his sports editor's position at the *Ottawa Citizen*. From then on, the former newspaperman's only "beat" would be hockey arenas. When the Senators were shut out of Cup action at the end of the 1921–22 season, perhaps Gorman wondered if his decision had been too hasty. Losing Jack Darragh was a blow; he'd decided it was time to retire. In his place, Gorman hired 18-year-old Ottawa phenomenon Frank Clancy. Soon the teenager's dash and flash earned him the nickname "King."

If Gorman had any regrets about leaving his newspaper job, the 1922–23 season put an end to them; the Senators' blitz resumed. Punch Broadbent and Cy Denneny — now dubbed the "gold dust twins" — finished first and second in the league's scoring race, racking up 59 of the team's 106 goals. Gorman was also successful in wooing Jack Darragh back into a Senator uniform for a final go-round. However, by the time the team boarded the train again to play the Vancouver Maroons — yes, the Senators were Cup finalists for the third time in four seasons — it was Darragh's turn to have second thoughts.

It had been a brutal season. By the time the team hit the ice in the finals, only three players remained uninjured. The list of afflictions read like a busy weekend in an emergency ward: a skull fracture, a bruised foot, facial lacerations, and a dislocated shoulder.

To add insult to injury, the ailing Senators had to play

two series against two teams. Their first objective: to win the best-of-five semifinals against the PCL Champions, the Maroons. Their second: to win a best-of-three against the Western Canada Hockey League's well-rested champs, the Edmonton Eskimos.

Once in Vancouver, the Senators accomplished their first objective in four games. Then, as if anxious to cut the agony short, the Senators quickly won the first two games against Edmonton, 2-1 and 1-0.

The last game was a typical demonstration of the team's never-give-an-inch defensive strategy. Ten minutes in, Broadbent scored the game's lone goal. That done, the Senators kept the Eskimos scoreless until the time ran out. Sometimes it seemed that half the team was slowly circling in the defensive zone.

If there was a series star, it was that newcomer, Frank Clancy. Taking over first from captain Eddie Gerard (laid low with his dislocated shoulder), Clancy then went on to play every defensive and forward position throughout the two games, even substituting for Clint Benedict while the goalie languished in the penalty box.

When the Senators finally arrived back home, it took 40 police officers to keep the crowd from suffocating the players. Frenzied fans virtually halted the 33-car parade, forcing bands that normally marched four abreast to worm their way through the throng single file.

Another season, another league championship. The

1923–24 season was good for Cy Denneny. His scoring ability earned him the Art Ross Trophy. Frank Nighbor was a winner, too. His 13 points in 20 games made him the first player to take home the League's new Hart Memorial (MVP) Trophy. However, Denneny, Nighbor, and the rest were unable to beat Montreal and a spiteful Sprague Cleghorn, who had been released by Gorman to the Canadiens in the wake of that brawl with the Vancouver Millionaires. The Senators lost both games of a two-game total-goal series. There would be no Stanley Cup. Jack Darragh decided to call it quits again and resume his retirement. And this time, he really meant it. The team never saw him again. Barely two months later, the entire hockey fraternity was stunned when Darragh died suddenly of acute peritonitis.

A Time of Change
The Senators' sit-on-the-lead defensive strategy helped win the team its Stanley Cups, but it didn't win over the press. Real hockey might be a lot of things, but it wasn't meant to be boring! The NHL was sensitive to the criticism. Besides, other teams were starting to catch on to the Senators' safe-and-sound playing methods. The NHL decided to inject some adrenaline into the game. It did so by legislating an anti-defence rule: when the puck left the defensive zone, no more than two defenders could stay behind.

  If the Senators were losing one advantage on the ice, they were about to gain two others, and one of them was the ice itself. The Senators couldn't increase ticket sales without a guarantee of good ice, and there were no guarantees when a hockey season stretched into early March. A brand new artificial ice venue would give them that guarantee. But Gorman and his partner, Ted Dey, couldn't do it alone. That meant another change. Gorman went looking for money and found Frank Ahearn.

The son of Thomas Franklin Ahearn, a trailblazing Ottawa engineer, debonair Frank Ahearn brought more than a love of hockey to the Senators when he entered into partnership with Gorman. He brought his family's fortune. When people jumped on one of Ottawa's clackity-clanging streetcars, they paid their fares to the Ahearns, who owned the system. More ladies were daring to walk after dark, bathed in the comforting glow of the streetlights planned and built by Thomas Ahearn. Now, with Gorman and his original partner, Dey, Frank Ahearn would own a piece of something else: a new artificial ice arena, the Ottawa Auditorium.

American businessmen in larger, warmer markets were watching. Artificial ice meant they could start cashing in on the NHL's growing popularity. Early in 1924, the NHL granted its first American franchise to a Boston grocery tycoon, Weston Adams. He called his team the Bruins. Before the next season even got underway, applications were received from New York, Philadelphia, and Pittsburgh. New York and Pittsburgh would play the next year. The league was expanding in Canada, too, with a second Montreal team.

The league's new teams needed players.

"How much?" the Montreal backers asked as they pointed to Punch Broadbent and Clint Benedict. A new Ottawa arena deserved a new, revitalized team. The Senators' second goalie, Alex Connell, was desperate for more playing time. The partners said goodbye to Benedict, Broadbent, and Lionel Hitchman (who joined the new Bruins). The Senators said hello to four new players, including exciting right wing prospect Reg "Hooley" Smith, and the kid they called the "Shawville Express": Frank Finnigan. The partners' decision had made young Finnigan's dream a reality, at last.

Ahearn and Gorman had dreams, too. They wanted more of the riches a bigger league and artificial ice promised. Ted Dey agreed to a buyout. When the 1924–25 season began, the Ottawa Senators were a Gorman-and-Ahearn show.

But as the season progressed, and Gorman watched the new teams (from bigger cities) perform, he felt an old familiar itch. He had been well aware of the increase in franchise value. That knowledge only intensified his itch to be a part of something bigger. In January 1925, he sold his share of the Senators to Ahearn, taking away $35,000 and Ahearn's interest in the Connaught Park Jockey Club. For the man who had initially been forced to borrow $2500 — half the team's price — to buy the team less than 10 years earlier, the Ottawa Senators had meant great fun, and great profit. But the team was the Frank Ahearn show now.

The Last Hurrah

Something was wrong. An astute businessman like Frank Ahearn could sense it. An analysis of the financial statements confirmed it: the Senators were losing money. How could this be? The team was winning games! True, the Senators had been edged out of the finals in the 1924–25 season, but that had to be expected as the team established its new, young players.

Still, the team's new additions developed fast. The Senators won 24 games in the 36 starts, giving the team the 1925–26 title. Although there was no Stanley Cup that year, Ahearn felt it was only a matter of time. When he looked at the gate receipts again, that nagging doubt persisted. Receipts down, costs up — those new players weren't cheap anymore.

Hockey was certainly booming. Another New York franchise, the Rangers, was in the works. Chicago and Detroit wanted in. Gorman was doing well, too. He was at Madison Square Garden now, helping establish the first New York franchise, the Americans. Indeed, hockey was hot. The 8000 fans that had poured into Ahearn's new Ottawa Auditorium in 1924 to watch the Stanley Cup final between Montreal and Calgary had proved it. But when hockey meant American teams, Ottawa fans didn't seem to care. What did these new teams have in common with them, after all? They were located in big cities — American cities a long way from Ottawa.

Ahearn, however, rarely let his worries show. He was a

wonderful owner and manager — the players all said so. They were champs and they were treated that way. "There was nothing but the best for us wherever we travelled," Frank Finnigan remembered decades later. "The best hotels, the best food … tickets for us to the best shows in New York, Chicago, Detroit …"

On the ice, the Senators continued to shine. League leaders in the 1926–27 season, they found themselves poised to bring home the Stanley Cup for a fourth time in a decade. Off the ice the shadow of insolvency lengthened. Even in this excellent season, the team often played before fewer than 3000 fans. Frank Ahearn lost $50,000, a huge loss at a time when ice cream was a nickel and a Tom Mix movie cost a dime. If the team won the Stanley Cup, wouldn't things turn around?

For the first time, the Senators travelled across the 49th parallel for Cup play. In Boston, they met the two-year-old Bruins, stars of the new American division. On one level, it was a disappointing series. Two scoreless games — the first and third in the series — were called at the end of overtime, when bad ice conditions contributed to the lack of scoring opportunities. Shockingly, that second scoreless game was in Ottawa's brand new, artificial ice arena.

The Senators took the next game 3-1, on goals by King Clancy, Denneny, and Finnigan. In the third period, game four, the play stopped and the fighting began as Hooley Smith attacked Boston's star right-winter Harry Oliver.

Ahearn was incensed. After the fighting — and the playing — was over, the scoreboard read Senators 3, Bruins 1. Winners of the O'Brien Cup, the NHL championship trophy, the Senators were automatically awarded the Stanley Cup. Soon after, Ahearn decided that Hooly Smith was history. It wasn't just the brawling, it was the bucks. Ahearn needed all the money he could get.

There was no parade that year for the "hometown heroes." Not enough people seemed to care. In fact, it was three weeks before a victory banquet was held at the Chateau Laurier, and when dinner was served, owner Frank Ahearn wasn't even there to enjoy it. He was in New York. And from there, he sent the revellers a bombshell. When the mayor read Ahearn's telegram aloud to 300 leading citizens and sports notables, a disturbed hush fell over the room. Ahearn made it official: the team was losing money and had been for years. He intended to sell his interest in the club. Though his surprised father, Thomas, tried to reassure the crowd, it was clear the dynasty days were over.

The end was painful and protracted. The Senators struggled on. The next season, the team dropped to third place in the Canadian division with only 20 wins. There was simply not enough of a solid, seasoned team left to put goals into the net and the Stanley Cup into the display case. By 1930, Ahearn had sold off Frank Nighbor and King Clancy. At the end of the 1933–34 season, the Senators finished dead last. Then, the name itself disappeared. The team went to

St. Louis, as the Eagles. After a dismal, one-season experience, the team folded.

League expansion, rising costs, and a city's unwillingness to embrace changes conspired to defeat the Ottawa Senators when, for 10 years, very little else ever did.

Fast-forward to 1990.

In West Palm Beach, Florida, NHL operators listened quietly while franchise hopefuls made their pitches. Then, it was Ottawa realtor Bruce Firestone's turn. Firestone laid out his plans. The numbers looked good. The planning had been thorough. The financial projections were convincing. It also seemed that this new team was part of hockey history. In recognition of that fabulous history, it would be called the Senators. As part of his contingent, Firestone brought along a white-haired 87-year-old gentleman who was a part of that history. "You're going to give those boys in Ottawa a chance," the older man demanded firmly.

NHL president John Ziegler allowed that he might. And he did.

Nobody was happier at the news of the successful bid for the new Ottawa Senators than that living link to an historical dynasty, the Shawville Express himself, Frank Finnigan.

Chapter 2
Montreal Canadiens
Stanley Cup Victories 1952–53,
1955–56, 1956–57, 1957–58,
1958–59, 1959–60

o begin to understand how it happened, how it *could* happen, you have to remember this: in the 1950s, hockey was simple. Playoffs? Two rounds of semifinals, then the best two teams were on to the Cup series. NHL hockey was simple because the NHL was small. There were just six teams. The league was actually one team smaller in 1950 than it was when World War II began — the Brooklyn Americans called it quits in 1942, a few months after Pearl Harbor. That happens when war robs a hockey league of over 80 players.

In the six-team league, there were three teams that were very strong and three that weren't. The strong ones: the

Detroit Red Wings, the Toronto Maple Leafs, and the Montreal Canadiens. The ones that weren't: the New York Rangers, the Chicago Blackhawks, and the Boston Bruins. If you are old enough to remember or fan enough to care, you might argue that there were *four* strong teams. You could make a case for Boston. The Bruins' two Stanley Cup finals (1957 and 1958) give you arguing rights. But that's it. And there was no Stanley Cup for the Bruins, either year. That wasn't Boston's fault, really — they were up against the Montreal Canadiens.

Were the Canadiens of the 1950s the greatest hockey team in history? Most hockey fans thought so, even then. Today, looking back at their record, many still feel that way.

Great Players
The Montreal Canadiens of the 1950s had great hockey players — an entire team of them. "We had everything," Hall of Famer center Jean Beliveau once recalled. "We had great scoring, we had checking, we had great goaltending. And we had great blending, the ideal combination of experienced veterans and good young rookies."

Beliveau was talking about Rocket Richard, Boom Boom Geoffrion, Dickie Moore, Doug Harvey, Jacques Plante, and at least a dozen others. As a Hart Trophy and Art Ross Trophy winner, and the very first recipient of the Conn Smythe Trophy, Le Gros Bill — as Beliveau's fans called him — was no slouch either. Thanks in part to his superb skating and stickhandling skills, the center celebrated 10 Stanley Cup wins. As general manager Frank Selke said at the time, Beliveau "is a perfect coach's hockey player, because he studies and learns. He's moving and planning all the time, thinking out the play required for each situation. Beliveau is a perfectionist; Richard is an opportunist."

Perhaps the top winger of his era (an era that included Gordie Howe), Maurice Richard was certainly the most exciting player in the game. However, Richard's early years were hardly spectacular, and he knew he wasn't the best skater in the league. He compensated for it with drive and determination, playing like a man possessed. No one played with more emotion.

In the jive-talk of the era, Richard was "the most." The man set many records: most NHL playoff goals, most goals in a single playoff year, most game-winning goals, and most consecutive games with goals. Ten years after he retired in 1961, all those records were still unbeaten. While he played, he was also the man most revered by Quebec fans, and the man most hated and feared by opponents. The record of 50 goals in 50 games that he set in his third year of professional hockey stood unchallenged for well over 30 years.

Bernie Geoffrion was nicknamed "Boom Boom" because of the sound that came when his blade hit the puck. Geoffrion simply lifted his stick like a golf club. It was different; it was deadly. They called it the slapshot. The puck wasn't the only thing Geoffrion knew how to hit. Outrageous

Bernie "Boom Boom" Geoffrion

and outgoing — a TV singing star in Quebec, no less — Boom Boom was suspended for eight games in 1953–54 when he sent the Rangers' Ron Murphy to the hospital. In the 1960–61 season, Geoffrion did what most would have thought impossible: the right winger became the second NHL player in history to score 50 goals in a season.

Who was the best? The Boomer? Rocket? Beliveau? People often asked Canadiens' 1960s superstar Yvan

Cournoyer that question. He would smile and admit that he couldn't say. "With the Canadiens, nobody was the best. We were taught it was a team game; a team effort."

During the fabulous '50s, there were outstanding players on other teams, of course. But the ones in Montreal were the best of the best — and there were so many of them; many more than on any other single team. How was that possible?

A Great System
At rinkside, frantic coaches tried to juggle their players to match the Habs' line changes. During key games, it seemed that a never-ending stream of fresh, energetic Canadiens rotated endlessly off the bench. The depth of the team — so *many* superb players — was among the toughest barriers to winning a game, let alone an entire playoff series, against Montreal. And it wasn't mere luck or coincidence that provided that depth.

Decades before he became a CBC icon, Peter Gzowski wrote this about the Montreal Canadiens: "One of the most remarkable facts about the team — and a tribute to [manager] Frank Selke's talent-seeking abilities — has been the way it has been able to refresh its strength from new, young players whenever a group of older ones begins to disintegrate."

The men who owned the Canadians did more than build a team. They built a system. In the days before the draft, NHL teams simply put the "new, young players" on protected lists and sent them off to play for junior teams. "Protecting" them was easy. The NHL allowed a team to claim a player by providing financial backing for his team. The Canadiens embraced the concept and created a huge cross-country farm team system.

South of the border, team operators grumbled; building a farm system was easy to do in hockey's snow-bound homeland, but not so easy to do in New York or Massachusetts. Eventually, Montreal had its pick of 10,000 players in 750 teams. It had created a player-producing system that was larger than that of all other NHL teams combined.

The Great Builders
The Hockey Hall of Fame honours not only great players, but also the outstanding owners, managers, and coaches who have created and guided the league's legendary teams. They are called the "builders." In the 1940s and 1950s, three master builders tore down and built up the team that became the benchmark of hockey excellence throughout the 1950s. All three would earn their right to be admitted to the Hall of Fame.

Wanted by slumping hockey team: an excellent, experienced coach.

As strange as it seems today, in 1940 the Canadiens were cellar-dwellers, finishing seventh in a seven-team league. Like the men he would mould into the finest hockey team in the land, debonair, silver-haired James Dickenson Irvin had been a hockey player, too — an English Canadian playing for the Montreal Maroons. His career cut short by a fractured skull, Dick Irvin became one of the game's first great coaches. He led the Toronto Maple Leafs for eight years, until his emotional, abrasive nature rubbed Leaf manager Conn Smythe the wrong way once too often.

Wanted by unemployed, but excellent, coach: a slumping hockey team.

The English-Canadian coach and *les Habitants* said "*bonjour.*" But there was no quick-and-easy turnaround, especially not for an English Canadian. Some in the French-language press demanded Irvin's dismissal. When one incensed Montrealer threatened to torch the Forum, it made headlines. Irvin had his players skate onto the ice wearing imitation firemen's hats.

The coach, however, wasn't always so light-hearted. He despised losing. One day, after a bout of bad shooting, Irvin had a goalie net dragged into the dressing room. He assembled his players and gave them a message that was short and sweet: "This is what the game is all about," he said, then tossed the puck into the net and walked out of the room. A conditioning advocate, Irvin's eagle eye would quickly spot any change in a player's waistline. He made it clear that either the flab went or the player did. In 1944, under Irvin, the Habs won the Stanley Cup for the first time since 1931. It was no fluke. They did it again in 1946.

Frank Selke, Montreal's manager, was, in one sense, a hockey "builder" long before he came to Montreal. In 1930, when Conn Smythe's vision of Maple Leaf Gardens was on the drawing boards (Smythe's Folly, they called it), his assistant, Selke, was instrumental in persuading Depression-ridden union construction workers to accept Gardens stock as part of their pay. A simmering feud with Smythe sent Selke, like Irvin before him, to Montreal. Selke had a new building project. He began construction of a Canadiens' farm-team system designed to feed Dick Irvin the potentially great players to develop around the team's leading star, the young Maurice Richard.

But by the mid 1950s, Dick Irvin was perceived by management as the spark that continually touched off Richard's explosive temper. If only they could control the Rocket better! Irvin's inflammatory behaviour wasn't helping, and both Selke and Irvin agreed that perhaps it would be best if the coach moved on. As he said goodbye and travelled to Chicago to coach the Blackhawks, no one knew Dick Irvin was dying of cancer.

Hector "Toe" Blake had been a hockey player, too, and an excellent one, starring with the Canadiens under Irvin's guidance. A Hart and Lady Byng Trophy winner, Blake finished first in scoring in 1940 — not easy to do when your team finishes last. As he would do a decade later around the Rocket, Dick Irvin had rebuilt that team around Toe Blake. Fiery and argumentative, Blake hated losing almost as much as Irvin did.

When he assumed his former coach's position, Toe

Blake remained just as intense, but more subtle — a rumbling, ominous volcano. After a defeat, players cringed when their coach walked into the dressing room, or when they were invited behind closed doors for a chat. Players — among the toughest in the league — would emerge from the office teary-eyed but grateful that Toe had given them "another chance." Unlike Irvin, Blake never berated his individual players publicly. He defended them, arguing with reporters on their behalf. In response, the players worked even harder for him. Pacing behind the bench in his suit and tie, fedora tilted high on his head, Blake was one of the most perceptive coaches in the game, surveying the action so skilfully that he unerringly knew just who to call in and just who to send out.

As much as the system, the builder, and the players, it was the team's collective will to win that set it apart. Canadien players who were traded were often shocked by the attitude they encountered in other teams. *Try* your best? We did *pretty* good? No wonder other teams got used to losing. In Montreal, winning was not just a good thing, it was everything. The Canadiens won for their city, for Toe, for their wives and kids. They won because it was expected. As Jean Beliveau said to newcomer Yvan Cournoyer, "At the end of the season we'll win the Stanley Cup and that's all that matters."

The Great Games
Where does one begin, when even the simple highlights of this team's history have filled entire books? Start with defeat.

Defeat can be the great destroyer, or a unifying force. There is a choice. The 1950s started badly, with Montreal out of the finals altogether. Next came two back-to-back Stanley Cup losses to two different teams, the Maple Leafs and the Red Wings. That 1951 Cup victory was to be the first and last of the decade for Toronto. As Toronto declined, Detroit ascended to dynasty status, powered by the so-called production line of center Sid Abel, Ted Lindsay, and Gordon Howe. Detroit welded itself in first place seven years in a row, with Howe as scoring champion four years straight. In 1953–54, the Rocket was runner-up — 14 points behind Howe.

Fourteen points behind the league-leading Red Wings (who had just beaten them soundly 5-0 in their final season game), the Canadiens fought their way to the finals by unexpectedly whipping Detroit in an exciting six-game series. Amazing! The first two games in Detroit were gruelling overtime marathons. In the first, it wasn't until the fourth overtime period that the Rocket scored the winning 3-2 goal. The second game remained scoreless until well into the third overtime period, when Richard beat Terry Sawchuck again. Rookie Gerry McNeil was in the net both times for Montreal. Especially thrilling was McNeil's game-saving lunge in game two. It was so unexpected that, for a second, a jubilant (and then crestfallen) Ted Lindsay actually thought he had put the puck in the net.

Rocket Richard scored 626 goals in his career. Among his most memorable was one he didn't really remember. In the seventh playoff game against Boston, in 1952, the Rocket tripped. On his knees, he was rammed by Bruins' Leo Labine. Revived by smelling salts, he was escorted off the ice. A cut over his left eye was stitched up and he was back on the bench. Was he okay to play? Irvin asked. Richard nodded and out he went. Late in the third period, the crowd's roar lifted the roof off the Forum: at an almost impossible angle, Richard had scored! The game was over and the team was off to the finals against Detroit. Later, reporter Elmer Ferguson was in the dressing room when Richard's father came in and gave his son a hug. The Rocket began to weep uncontrollably. The reporter was stunned. It was then he realized, "That beautiful bastard scored semi-conscious."

The next season, the Canadiens would be denied the Cup no longer. Nor would one Canadiens' veteran, whose career was soon to end in well-earned retirement. Elmer Lach would bow out in fine style. The Canadiens faced Boston, who had just shut down Detroit in the semifinals. "I don't see how we can even win a single game," sighed Dick Irvin. His team showed him how, winning game one 4-2. Boston came back 4-1 in game two. Gerry McNeil shut out the Bruins 3-0 in game three, and Montreal added insult to injury by beating Boston 7-3 in game four.

A scoreless game five was in sudden-death overtime when the 35-year-old Lach saw the puck come out from behind the Boston net and bounce on his stick. He didn't even think. He just turned around and fired. Players flattened themselves, desperate to stop the puck. The red light went on. The Canadiens had won the game and the Stanley Cup. It was a wonderful moment for the team and for Lach. It might have been even better if Rocket Richard hadn't jumped into Lach's arms and broken his teammate's nose.

Another pair of Stanley Cup losses to Detroit laid the Canadiens low. The first defeat came after a fiercely fought seven-game final series. Neither team scored more than two goals in each of the last four games. The deciding came on a weak, slow shot from Detroit's Tony Leswick. Doug Harvey tried to stop it with his glove, but instead, he merely deflected it and then it somehow eluded goalie Gerry McNeil. That shot broke a tie, the heart of every Canadien fan, and that of McNeil, who hung up his skates for good. The shadow of that goal followed him the rest of his life.

Sometimes the lessons of defeat are extremely hard. The lesson of the 1954–55 season that was to change the team's fortunes and Maurice Richard's career had its climax just four games from the end of the season. At that moment, it appeared that Richard just might win the scoring championship. Instead, what awaited him was the most famous fight — and punishment — in hockey history.

Playing against Boston late in the third period with the Bruins leading, Richard highsticked Boston defenceman Hal Laycoe. Laycoe — a friend of Richard's — then whacked him over the head with his stick. Blood ran. Tempers exploded. Sticks began swinging. Maddened, perhaps, by the sight of

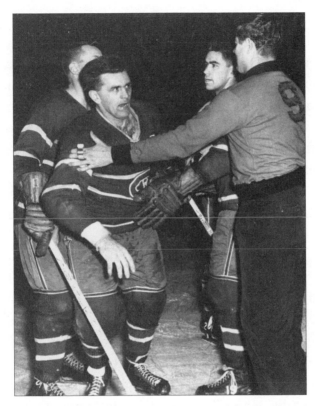

Linesman George Hayes restrains Maurice Richard after being
boarded by Bob Bailey of the Maple Leafs in December 1954

his own blood, Richard went berserk. In moments he was
fighting linesman Cliff Thompson. Close to 14,000 fans sat in
shocked silence. By the time it was all over, half the crowd
was gone. They knew they had witnessed something very dis-
turbing. Someone else sitting in the stands came to the same

conclusion — NHL President Clarence Campbell.

Just before Christmas, pressured by other league governors, Campbell had called Selke and Richard to his office over
another fighting incident that had led to a major and two
misconduct penalties. This time, the penalty would be more
severe and Montreal manager Frank Selke knew it. He understood the pressure Campbell was under from other governors
and team managers, especially Detroit's belligerent Jack
Adams. A hearing was held. Selke didn't even attend. He knew
only too well what was going to happen. Richard was suspended for the rest of the season — and the playoffs, too.

Inflammatory press fuelled the fires of outrage.
Demonstrations began the afternoon of the next Montreal-
Detroit game in the Montreal Forum. Worse, Clarence
Campbell decided to attend the game. Only an exploding
tear-gas bomb dissuaded a mob from tearing him limb from
limb. For a time, Campbell hid out in the first-aid room (ironically, so did the Rocket and his wife, Lucille, who had been
watching the game). Then, smeared by tomatoes and eggs,
the president of the NHL escaped quietly into the night. In
the now-legendary "Richard Riot" that followed, the city was
trashed for blocks. Urged on by Dick Irvin, Richard sat before
a small forest of radio station microphones and called for
calm. It was all he could do. He was through for the season.
So were the Canadiens.

"Without Richard, the team had lost its soul," Frank
Selke remembered in his autobiography. "Our boys were

certain that, in one fell stroke, they had lost both the league championship and the Stanley Cup." A self-fulfilling prophecy. Beaten by Detroit, the Canadiens placed second. There was no second-best in the finals that followed; a team either won or lost. The Canadiens lost the Cup. Then, they lost their coach. Frank Selke felt Dick Irvin had goaded Richard into violence far too long. He told his friend he could stay with the Canadiens, but not as coach. However there was a coaching position available in Chicago …

As the season ended for Maurice Richard, so, too, did one of his cherished dreams, shattered by a close friend and teammate. During Richard's suspension, the Boomer surpassed the Rocket's record and became scoring champion. "I couldn't deliberately not score," Bernie Geoffrion explained.

Richard's fiercely loyal Montreal fans were outraged. Geoffrion's life became a nightmare. Threats were made. He asked for police protection for his wife and children. Sickened, he thought seriously about quitting hockey. Although sick at heart himself, Maurice Richard visited Geoffrion and, along with Jean Beliveau, convinced him to stay with the team.

There were meetings with Maurice Richard, too, the following summer. Frank Selke and new coach Toe Blake met with Richard a number of times before the season began, calming him; the important thing, they emphasized again and again, was not one game or one fight, it was to lead the team to the Stanley Cup.

At the training camp, Blake could see that the team was forging an enormously strong will to recover from their losses, not only their loss of the Stanley Cup, but their loss of face in the public's eye. "They were determined. They were not going to let anything beat them this time," Blake recalled, "least of all themselves."

The comeback strength was deep, three lines deep: a Richard line, a Beliveau line, and then the backup line with a number of combinations, including Claude Provost. The Canadiens' devastating power play would score 25 percent of the team's goals. Toe didn't try to change his players' style. With so many superstars in the ranks (10 playing that year would become Hall of Famers), why not just let them go? However, he told them, "Four or five stars don't make a team." Everyone who put on a uniform was important.

And so, the greatest dynasty of all came to be. The CBC underestimated the fans' fervour for a Montreal Cup win and announced it would only carry Cup games that were played on its regular *Hockey Night In Canada*, on Saturday evenings. That night, over 1000 phone calls persuaded the network to change its mind: all games would be televised.

In the final against the Red Wings, Jean Beliveau scored seven times and Jacques Plante allowed only five goals in the final four of the five games. Late in game five, as Dink Carroll of the *Montreal Gazette* reported, "The lightning of Montreal's famed power play struck with devastating effectiveness twice within 52 seconds and the Red Wings were dead." As the siren sounded to end the game, Canadiens swarmed Plante. Toe Blake was hoisted on the shoulders of Plante and Boom Boom as the crowd sang "For He's A Jolly Good Fellow." Captain Butch Bouchard made a tour of the rink with the Cup. The next day, it took a 4-band, 6-float, and 35-car parade over 6 hours to snake its way down a 50-kilometre route as thousands swarmed the street.

A few new players — Henri "Pocket Rocket" Richard, Ralph Backstrom, Bert Olmstead, and Bobby Rousseau — put on the Canadiens' colours as the decade advanced. Essentially, though, it was the same team — the same winners — from the early 1950s who led the team to glory in the late '50s and even into the early '60s. Between 1956 and 1960, Montreal rarely met a serious challenge during the playoffs, winning 40 of 49 games against every other NHL team. Those games were won by the same legendary hockey heroes who then led the team to that never-to-be-surpassed record: five Stanley Cup victories in a row.

Chapter 3
Toronto Maple Leafs
Stanley Cup Victories: 1961–62, 1962–63, 1963–64, 1966–67

B y the dawn of the 1960s, the Toronto Maple Leafs were the most popular sports team in Canada. In some ways, that sway over the game went far beyond victories the team celebrated and trophies its players won. The Maple Leafs influenced hockey on many levels: how it was organized and managed, how it was played, how it was heard and viewed by its millions of fans across the country, and even, in an earlier age, how the game was watched from rinkside.

In 1931, at a time when the claws of the Depression clutched at everyone's wallet, Conn Smythe, the Leafs' new owner, found $1.5 million and built Canada's largest arena for the team to play in. Inside the Maple Leaf Gardens, not a single pillar obstructed the wonderful sight of the brand new home team as it fought for, and won, the Stanley Cup against the New York Rangers. In that pre-television age, the Leafs and the palace they played in became almost mythical, thanks to the radio broadcasts of Foster Hewitt. (Hewitt, Mister "He-shoots-he-scores," was a Smythe idea, too.) The Leafs were more than a hockey team. People called them an empire, one that still dominated decades later.

Like their hated rivals, the Montreal Canadiens, the Leafs created an efficient, effective hockey-player manufacturing arm: the minor-league network. Each team acted as a "branch plant," creating the "product" that fed the club's insatiable appetite for great players. The New York Rangers began the decade with just two junior teams. Montreal had 18. Little wonder the Habs and Leafs were the league's most powerful units. Owners and operators of American teams complained that NHL rules gave Canadian teams new-player advantages.

Bitter Rivalry

Talk about dominating the decade! The Toronto Maple Leafs and the Montreal Canadiens won nine of the ten Stanley Cups between 1960 and 1969. You might as well include 1959 in the decade, too, when for the first time in eight seasons the two teams fought each other for the Cup. When fans thought back, it was the only truly fitting climax to the Leafs' 1958–59 season. That year was the start of something, all right. The "something" was George "Punch" Imlach, a bald, middle-aged man with the nondescript mantle of assistant general manager. First impressions can be misleading. He walked in from nowhere (well, Quebec actually, where he coached minor hockey) and a few months later he was manager. Not bad for a guy without major league experience, on or off the ice.

The players discovered that Imlach was brash and cocky. They liked that — at first. Over the next few short months, Punch would galvanize the team and turn them into Cup contenders. *Everybody* liked that.

Imlach bolstered the team's defence with canny trades, adding Carl Brewer and Allan Stanley (already over 30 years of age) to play alongside Tim Horton and Bob Baun. It didn't seem to help. After 15 losses and just 5 wins, the frustrated manager quietly canvassed individual players. Would they back him as coach? The answer was yes. In a move that had jaws dropping all around town, Punch fired coach Billy Reay and appointed himself as Reay's replacement. Players responded positively to Imlach's "take charge" attitude. The man had confidence in himself, no question ("Rather be shot for a lion than a lamb," Imlach roared to the *Globe* a few hours after Reay left), but Imlach made it just as obvious to the players that he had confidence in *them*. For the moment.

Nevertheless, it was uphill all the way. In March 1959, with just five games remaining, the Leafs sat in last spot, seven points back of the Rangers. Making sudden rinkside decisions — crazy, showboat decisions — Imlach inspired four crucial wins in a row from his team. On the last day of the regular season, the Leafs played Detroit. Behind 2-0 at the end of the first period, captain George Armstrong told Imlach, "We'll get it for you." And they did, winning the game 6-4. Indeed, something was happening.

Montreal defeated Toronto in the five-game Cup series, but what was important was that the Leafs actually got to play it. "After 1959," forward Billy Harris remembered, "there was a feeling it was just a matter of time before we won everything."

First, there was some team-building to be done. The Leafs had strengths, but, obviously, not enough. Imlach brought in one-time Red Wing star defenceman, Red Kelly. Detroit wanted youth. Kelly, by then 32 years old, didn't qualify. Imlach didn't care.

The Leafs' fortunes improved in the 1959–60 season. The team finished second, with 53-26-9. The Toronto-Montreal rivalry intensified. Once again, the Stanley Cup beckoned. Once again, Toronto faced Montreal. It was a grudge match — all Leafs-Habs games were grudge matches.

"Oh, I loved going in there to play against Toronto," Montreal Canadiens forward John Ferguson told author Stephen Cole. "Those games were wars. They hated us. We hated them." Once again, the Cup series brought defeat for Toronto, this time in just four games. That meant more changes.

The next season, new players were brought in on trades and moved up from the minor hockey system. Ranger Eddie Shack came aboard, his tough and unpredictable behaviour a motivating force on the team's third line. Two newcomers arrived, Bob Nevin and little Dave Keon (Keon would win the Calder Trophy as top rookie). Nevin moved to right wing. Imlach shifted Kelly up from defence to center ice, where he became a star, the playmaker for left-winger Frank Mahovlich, the "Big M," who had a stellar 1960–61 season with a club record of 48 goals. Second line: Keon at center, Dick Duff on the left side, and George Armstong on the right. They called Armstrong "the Chief," a nickname that had much more to do with his Ojibway heritage than it did his position as captain. Johnny Bower and Don Simmons were the Leafs' netminders.

Johnny Bower had joined the team in that auspicious 1958–59 season, after 15 years in the minors. It was tough to be a standout in the net during an era of goalie greats such as Jacques Plante (Montreal), Glenn Hall (Chicago), and Terry Sawchuk (Detroit). However, in spite of formidable competition — and a leg injury that sidelined him for 12 games — the fiercely competitive Bower managed to win the Vezina Trophy as the league's best goalie in the 1960–61 season. Bower didn't need the trophy to convince Punch Imlach of his worth. The coach felt the netminder's absence had cost the team the league championship, and was the reason they were eliminated in the first round playoffs. For a team that

Frank "Big M" Mahovlich

fought its way to a second-place finish just two points behind the Canadiens, it was a sad way to end a season.

The Work Ethic Gone Mad

Painted near the ceiling of the Leafs' dressing room, above the shelf and hooks where pads and gloves were stored, were the words: THE PRICE OF SUCCESS IS HARD WORK.

Under Punch Imlach, the price paid by the players was steep. Work? Imlach brought a new, exhausting meaning to the four-letter word. Practices were gruelling marathons, punctuated by Punch's top-of-the-lungs epithets. Not one practice a day, but *two*, often hours long each. "[Imlach] worked us into the ground, really," was the way the Big M remembered it. The players were almost as tough on each other as Imlach was on them, incurring as many injuries during training as they suffered by mid-season from opposing teams. The Chief seemed to personify Imlach's work ethic. Low on natural ability, Armstrong scored high in effort. He was a conscience-on-skates for some of the others.

After training camp came pre-season exhibition games. All teams played them, but the Leafs played more. In 1964, the team endured 18 matches in 30 days — eight of them in just two weeks. Who could blame Tim Horton and Bob Pulford for "trashing" Quebec City's Grand Allee during a 1963 exhibition stopover? The offence: kicking over garbage cans. The fine: $50 each.

The price of success may have been hard work, but the price of failure was far worse. It came with abject humiliation, punctured pride, and bruised dignity. The victories belonged to Punch Imlach. The defeats belonged to "my bums." The haranguing coach sometimes treated his younger players viciously, but no one suffered more than veteran winger Frank Mahovlich. True, the Big M could be infuriating to coach and fans alike. In one game he looked like a star. In the next he looked like a snoozing slacker. Still, this seemed like a poor excuse for the way Punch picked on Mahovlich mercilessly — and publicly. Talking to the press, it seemed that Imlach loved to denigrate the man, deliberately and repeatedly mispronouncing his name. "Ma-holo-vich," he would sneer. Was he really trying to goad the Big M into better performance? If so, by 1964, the tactic had backfired. Mahovlich spiralled downward into clinical depression.

Imlach was a driven disciplinarian. He didn't spare his players. Nor did he spare himself. In that, Punch Imlach earned his players' respect, but his tirades and taunts cost him their affection. Heartless? Maybe. Effective? Well, somebody was responsible for taking the team to the playoffs every year for eight years. And somebody was responsible for inspiring the team to win the Cup four of those eight times.

Cup Fever

Imlach vowed there would be no playoff collapse in 1962. The team responded, and went out and beat the New York Rangers in six games. Toronto was jubilant. It was time — at last — to play for the Stanley Cup against the Cup-holders who had beaten the Red Wings in the finals the year before: the Chicago Blackhawks.

The series opened in Toronto, and, perhaps inspired by the rabid hometown fans, the Leafs took the first two games. In game one, the Blackhawks tried hard to take the game into the Toronto end, but as their captain, Pierre Pilote, moaned, "We ran out of gas." Winning score: 4-1. In game two, the Leafs had plenty of high-octane left, and drove the Hawks out of Toronto with a 3-2 win. Never mind, predicted a stoic Bobby Hull, the Blackhawks would tie the series up on home ice. Sure enough, Chicago shut out the Maple Leafs 3-0 in game three and just missed another shutout in game four, with the final 4-1 score celebrated in a shower of toilet paper, fruit, and hats thrown from the stands.

Back in Toronto, the raucous gang in the Gardens was not to be outdone; the ice was littered. The game itself was penalty-strewn. Seventeen minors and two ten-minute misconducts were served. Five minute slashing majors were levied against both Toronto's Frank Mahovlich and Chicago's Stan Mikita. Hard-fought to the bitter end, the game was Toronto's by a healthy 8-4 margin. The teams then travelled back to Chicago for game six.

There, the two teams battled it out for almost 50 scoreless minutes. Then, Bobby Hull's shot on goal spun off goalie Don Simmons' left leg and into the net. In the time it took to clear the debris off the ice, the shaken Toronto squad regrouped. Bob Nevin tied the score, and then Tim Horton passed to Dick Duff, who shot the puck past Chicago goalie Glenn Hall. And the Leafs kissed the Cup for the first time since 1951. Two days later, in what the *Toronto Star* called "the greatest reception in Stanley Cup history," an estimated 100,000 delirious fans lined the parade route to City Hall. For their next trick, the Leafs hosted the 1962 All-Star game and won that, too, 4-1.

In 1963, the Maple Leafs earned themselves first place in the league, a feat they had not achieved in 15 years. They then held the Canadiens to just five goals in the five-game playoff series. Imlach was confident of beating Detroit in the finals. "I don't think Detroit has three centers to match Keon, Kelly and (Bob) Pulford," he boasted. "Show me where they have five defencemen as good as the five I can put out on the ice."

But would Toronto's stronger defencemen guarantee a Stanley Cup? The newshounds could be forgiven a healthy skepticism. After all, Detroit's Gordie Howe and Norm Ullman were leading playoff scorers, with 16 points each. But the Leafs' Johnny Bower would be in front of the net. No puck would pass unchallenged. In fact, most wouldn't pass at all. Bower would only allow 16 goals in 10 playoff games.

And so it was that the Leafs quickly posted a pair of 4-2 hometown Cup series victories, with Dick Duff scoring twice 70 seconds into game one. Back in Detroit, game three was a do-or-die effort on the part of the Red Wings. They had just one man to thank for their 3-2 win: rookie center Alex Faulkner. Surprisingly, it was Faulkner who scored two goals, including the final marker. Even more amazing, it was his third winning goal of the playoffs. In game four, Toronto's Dave Keon broke a 2-2 tie and Kelly added another goal to give Toronto a comfortable win.

Most of game five was a close 1-1 contest. It was a painful contest for Carl Brewer, as the doctor sewed 10 stitches into his mouth. With less than seven minutes remaining, Eddie Shack was standing near the Detroit goal when the puck hit his stick and simply slipped into the net. For Brewer, things went from bad to worse when his arm was broken two minutes later. But Maple Leaf Dave Keon had a great night. He scored his second goal of the game and the Leafs won their second consecutive Stanley Cup for — again — the first time in 15 years. "Wee Davie" won his second Lady Byng Trophy and Frank Mahovlich, who scored 36 goals in the season, once more made the All-Star team.

All Work, Little Play

The 1963–64 season started well for Toronto. Then things fell apart. The familiar Maple Leafs, league champs and two-time Cup winners, simply disappeared. In their place skated players in blue-and-white Toronto uniforms who couldn't score, coached by a tortured screamer whose apoplectic rages knew no bounds. Fans booed when the Leafs lost to the Canadiens in November and again in January. In one game during the season, Boston annihilated Toronto 11-0.

A depressed Mahovlich checked himself into the hospital, and disgusted defenceman Carl Brewer refused to sign his contract. The reason wasn't Imlach's tirades, but his parsimonious penny-pinching. As he had the year before, Brewer hit the books on campus. And also like the year before, he allowed himself to be coaxed back with bigger bucks — danger pay, perhaps, to compensate for the previous season's punishing finals.

To turn the team around, Imlach went big-player hunting. He had offensive dynamo Andy Bathgate in his sights. It had been five years — a sporting eternity — since the New York Ranger had been MVP. Now Bathgate was 31. As usual, that didn't bother Punch. He preferred seasoned veterans. Defenceman Red Kelly, a 33-year-old player presumably past his prime, had found new energy in his new position at center. "The old players are the best," Punch said knowingly. "Each one of them has tremendous desire."

Imlach had desire, too — the desire to bag Bathgate. It took five players to do it: Duff and Nevin, Bill Collins (from the minors), and two other young defencemen. Bathgate, who came with center Don McKenney, was slotted with Kelly and Mahovlich. By the time the playoffs arrived, the Leafs redeemed themselves by finishing third. Even better, they won a best-of-seven semifinal series against the Canadiens. In the 3-1 final game, Dave Keon scored all three goals. The Maple Leafs would reacquaint themselves with the Detroit Red Wings in Stanley Cup play.

Both clubs entered the series exhausted. Toronto somehow won the first game 3-2. There was no respite; no reward. Imlach worked the team hard at a full practice for game two, while Detroit players went sightseeing and played the ponies at the Fort Erie racetack. Refreshed, the Red Wings controlled much of game two, and had a one-goal lead 43 seconds from the end of the third period. Jerry Ehman tied it up at 3-3. In front of the Toronto goal, Gordie Howe slid the puck to Larry Jeffrey, who snapped it in. The game was Detroit's. The next day, while the Leafs practised hard and studied films of their latest defeat, Red Wingers had more fun at the track. When the teams hit the ice, it was the same story and the same score. Toronto tied it up 3-3 in the third, but Howe stole the puck from Mahovlich, and passed to Alex Delvecchio who delivered the 4-3 winning goal.

In game four, Toronto evened the series out at 2-2. In game five — after another strenuous practice — the Leafs took an early lead on the strength of breakaways from Keon and Mahovlich. However, the Red Wings stole the show and won 4-2. There was a lot riding on game six for Detroit: the team's first Cup in nine years. More than 15,000 fans jammed The Olympia. The game was tied 3-3 with less than seven minutes on the clock when a Hollywood screenplay finish unfolded. Detroit's Alex Delvecchio fired a hard, low scream-er that fractured Bobby Baun's right ankle. Baun was carried off on a stretcher. "Gimme a shot," he yelled at his doctors. In less than five minutes he was on his feet and on the ice. It was overtime now. Baun fired the puck. It struck the stick of Detroit defenceman Bill Gadsby, rebounding across the ice and into the net behind an incredulous Terry Sawchuk. The Leafs won 4-3.

In game seven, Bobby Baun skated onto the ice of

Maple Leaf Gardens, his leg novocained up to his hip. Red Kelly popped painkillers to ward off the agony of twisted knee ligaments. Syringes were emptied into Carl Brewer to dull the ache of damaged ribs, and into George Armstrong so he could move his shoulder. Newcomer Andy Bathgate put the Leafs on the scoreboard, but it was Johnny Bower who gave them their Cup-winning 4-0 shutout. Two hours after the gleeful Toronto players showered each other with champagne, Kelly was on his way to the hospital, smiling through the pain.

One More Year of Glory
In 1960, the Leafs had lost a second Stanley Cup in a row to the Montreal Canadiens in a quick, savage, four-game series. This disappointment, and Montreal's soon-to-be-legendary status as the only team to win five straight Stanley Cups, merely intensified the enmity in Toronto and wherever Leafs fans fumed. The combined psychic vibrations of these millions went out into the ether: *Just give 'em another chance, just one more chance.*

The hockey fates were listening. They decreed that the two teams would wage Stanley Cup warfare once more during the decade. Any Stanley Cup series is a special event. However, the extreme emotions generated by a Leafs-Canadiens Cup contest always catapulted the finals to the very highest plane of excitement. Even those who ignored hockey all year long got fired up.

It would be a Cup series between two traditional combatants — the 13th playoff series capping virtually a half-century of sometimes-bitter rivalry. These games would represent other rivalries: the rivalry between French and English Canadians; between the country's two largest cities; between a team of style and finesse (Montreal) and one of dogged determination (Toronto). So, if the Leafs and the Habs were going to tangle for the Cup, it was only fitting that the match-up should take place during a very special year. The fates consulted the future and agreed that the next Cup "summit meeting" between the league's two top teams would be held during the NHL's 50th anniversary year, 1967.

That year would be Canada's centennial year. It would also be the year of Expo; of futuristic Habitat and that glistening dome on Montreal island; the year we Canadians sang, "Ca-a-a-na-a-a-da," the hit song written and performed by Canada's Pied Piper, Bobby Gimby. It would also become a cultural turning point, the year of the Summer of Love, flower power, and the pulsing sounds of musical trendsetters such as Jefferson Airplane and the Grateful Dead. It would be the year of a "youth-quake" that sent out the aftershocks of sex, drugs, and rock'n'roll.

The hockey fates had made another momentous decision, one that would not be revealed until 1965. The fates were teases; they couldn't resist giving us a hint. In the summer of 1960, they had arranged a pair of pre-season games between the Leafs and Boston. Yeah, so what? But wait,

they're playing where? *Los Angeles*? That was interesting —
anything the Leafs did was interesting, but few realized the
significance of that far-flung West Coast location, or that
crowds watching the games were larger than some expected.

The fates would compel the small, intimate, six-team
National Hockey League to finally embrace expansion —
which would include Los Angeles — at the end of the 1966–67
season. Call it a fateful decision. The final game of the 1967
Stanley Cup series would be more than the finale of another
hockey season. It would signal the end of an era. What a cos-
mic concept: the Leafs and Habs — two top Canadian teams
— fighting it out in Stanley Cup competition during Canada's
— and hockey's — most momentous year. No other teams
would do. No other time would be so right.

In 1965 and 1966, the Over-The-Hill-Gang didn't even
make the playoffs. Ironically, Carl Brewer — at 27, one of the
younger of the bunch — was the one who retired. Many he
left behind had earned the right to join him; Johnny Bower
was 42, defenceman Allan Stanley was 41, forward Red Kelly
was 39, center George Armstrong was 37, and forward Bob
Pulford was 31. Some newcomers weren't "new" at all. One,
former Canadiens star Dickie Moore, was on the comeback
trail. The young-thinking Red Wings left Terry Sawchuck
unprotected during the 1964 draft. Rookie of the year in 1951,
37-year-old Sawchuck was old bones, but brilliant: a three-
time Cup winner and four-time Vezina Trophy holder. Imlach
snapped him up.

In the 1966–67 season, a 10-game slump left the team in fifth place. Sawchuck was so miserable in his new, losing club that he considered quitting. "Worst run I've ever had in hockey," Punch confessed to the newspapers. He was desperate for a plan. He tried everything.

The Stanley Cup? It looked like these old coots wouldn't even see the playoffs, Torontonians scoffed. Just like the year before. And just like the year before that. In early February, the team finally managed a 4-4 tie against Chicago's mighty Mikita line. It was the turning point. A three-game streak quickly followed. Toronto was back.

But Punch Imlach felt lousy; there was pain in his chest and arm. One night he called King Clancy from the hospital. "They got me locked up. Will you run the club tonight?"

"What's wrong?" reporters asked.

"Exhaustion," doctors said.

"How long?" they pressed.

"At least two weeks," Clancy answered. For Leafs lifer King Clancy, a 1920s star, 1950s coach, and now front-office favourite, it felt like old times. It felt that way to the players, too.

"[Clancy] just let the reins go," Eddie Shack recalled. "Everybody did what came naturally … it was fantastic."

The three-game streak was followed by a three-week streak; seven wins in ten games. Go, Leafs, go! By season's end, the geriatric set was in a third place best-of-seven playoff spot against the Chicago Blackhawks. The Hawks had enjoyed a tremendous season. Billy Reay, the Leafs coach so unceremoniously dumped by Punch Imlach, now coached the Chicago juggernaut. How he must have gloated.

Minutes into the fifth game, Bobby Hull swung around to his left and whacked the puck. Terry Sawchuck stopped it just under his neck and crashed to the ice, unconscious. Rousing himself after a minute or so, Sawchuk instinctively picked up his stick. Trainer Bob Haggert ran out onto the ice.

Haggert to Sawchuck: "Are you all right?"

Sawchuck to Haggert: "I stopped the damn shot, didn't I?"

Sawchuck went on to stop another 22 shots in the game. In spite of all the firepower of Esposito, Mikita, and Hull (who alone had scored more goals that season than the two top Leaf scorers combined), Sawchuck and Bower allowed the Blackhawks just eight goals in six games. It was time for the ultimate Leafs-Canadiens Cup contest.

Both teams had scores to settle. In 1963 and 1964, the Canadiens had sat solemnly in front of their television sets, watching Toronto win the Stanley Cup. The next two years, the Leafs had sat in front of their television sets, watching the Canadiens win the Cup. At the Canadiens' long-awaited 1965 victory reception, Montreal's mayor, Jean Drapeau, had told the team, "When you win your third cup in a row, we can give you an absolutely tremendous reception at the World's Fair." Oh yes, this one was going to be special.

In game one, an abject Terry Sawchuk was pulled after

letting in four goals in the first two periods. Montreal master-minded a 6-2 win. Canadiens fans wondered if it was going to that easy. No way. In game two a bleeding and battered Johnny Bower coolly shut out the Canadiens 3-0 in the Montreal Forum, and then, back in the Gardens, held off the Habs in game three to ensure Toronto a 3-2 overtime win. In game four, the Canadiens came back 6-2 on great saves by rookie netminder Rogatien Vachon. Again, Sawchuck gave up a loss. The series was tied 2-2.

In game five, in the Forum, goaltending was the deciding factor once again. Pointing at Vachon, Punch Imlach announced that no Junior B goalie was going to beat his team. Montreal scored first, but couldn't build their traditional momentum and Toronto tied it up. Then the Leafs moved ahead on a goal by Brian Conacher, and further ahead with others by Marcel Pronovost and Dave Keon. Montreal replaced the rattled Vachon with Gump Worsley, but it was already over. Toronto concentrated on hanging onto that 4-1 lead and turned it into the final score.

A more confident Terry Sawchuk was Toronto's starter in game six at the Gardens. He was formidable, stopping 17 shots in the first period to keep the Canadiens scoreless. "The game was so tense," sportswriter Dick Beddoes put it, "you could've grated carrots on the fans' goosebumps." Leafs led 2-0 going into the third period. Former Leaf Dick Duff closed the gap with a goal for the Canadiens. It was 2-1. Then Toronto's Hillman iced the puck. Millions watched Toe Blake bench goalie Gump Worsley to provide an extra attacker. With just 55 seconds to play, this special season, the coveted Stanley Cup, a half-century of rivalry, and an entire NHL era, came down to a single, fatal face-off in the Maple Leaf zone. For Montreal it was Jean Beliveau. Imlach re-jigged his line and said "Stanley, you take the face-off."

Allan Stanley couldn't believe it. It had been four years since he'd taken a face-off. "Me? Against *Jean Beliveau*?" Typical Imlach: another showboat move. But why now?

Out on the ice, Stanley told Red Kelly to line up slightly behind him because that's where he was going to put the puck. Stanley did exactly what he said he'd do, charging at a stunned Beliveau. When the puck rolled his way, Kelly was ready. He moved it up to Pulford, who gave it to George Armstrong. The empty net awaited. The Chief took a simple, elementary wrist shot. Final score: 3-1.

Montreal hosted the world at Expo '67. Toronto settled for a Stanley Cup parade. The 30,000 people who lined the parade route thought that was just fine.

Chapter 4
Philadelphia Flyers
Stanley Cup Victories: 1973–74,
1974–75

n the arena stands, fans stared open-mouthed as even more players were ordered off the ice. At home, sitting otherwise comfortably in their easy chairs, television viewers winced and shook their heads. So this was hockey!

The Broad Street Bullies: The Team They Loved to Hate

"Broad Street" was where Philadelphia's Spectrum, home-ice of the Philadelphia Flyers, stood. "Bullies" was the tag earned for the rough, tough, penalty-ridden hockey the team played in the 1970s. If names meant anything — and with this squad, they meant plenty — monikers such as "Moose," "Cowboy," "Hotdog," and "The Hammer" gave the innocent and the unknowing a hint of what they were about to see.

Philadelphia Flyers: 1973–1975

In the 1973–74 season, while on their way to their first Cup victory, the Flyers earned the dubious distinction of becoming penalty league-leaders, earning a stunning 1754 minutes. Two seasons later, left-winger Dave "The Hammer" Schultz earned a season record in penalties for a single player as he sat out 472 minutes in the box. "Hockey is a contact sport. It's not the ice follies," Schultz explained bluntly. Was this the same Dave Schultz who had grown up in a Mennonite community and attended Bible camp in the summertime? Indeed it was.

Captain Bobby Clarke earned his own share of notoriety. "The dirtiest player in hockey," sneered Canadiens coach Scotty Bowman.

Hockey had never been a "nice" game. For decades, players — even coaches and managers — had come out swinging. Blood on the ice, deft stitching in the dressing room, and quick ambulance trips to the hospital didn't suddenly start with the league's expansion after the 1966–67 season. However, it seemed that this was the first time hot tempers were replaced by a kind of cool and deliberate mayhem that both shocked and thrilled fans.

There were also many superheated moments in which the fighting was sudden and unplanned, a reaction to the craziness of others. During one brawl, an overzealous spectator decided to become a participant, tugging on the hair of forward Don Saleski. That act brought quick retaliation. Skates and all, players thumped their way up into the stands to mete out some Flyers-style retribution from the misguided fan. The Flyers' rough stuff started earning players more than penalty points and public outcries. It earned them criminal charges brought by none other than Ontario's Attorney General.

But maybe, some argued, the escalating violence was merely perception. The mounting level of adverse publicity was certainly no illusion, but perhaps the public's concern was misplaced. Perhaps the criticism wasn't so much about the violence as it was about its sudden accessibility. There it was, in our homes, right on television. What was it doing to the kids?

What gave the criticism its momentum was the fact that, quite suddenly, the league's first expansion and the subsequent growth of the "other" league, the World Hockey Association (WHA), created professional teams in such unlikely places as Georgia, Missouri, California, and Texas. Professional hockey — and the violence that had always been part of the game — was introduced in large cities where few had ever seen hockey and many still associated the game with faraway places that endured months of ice and snow.

In creating more teams the league also created something else: a huge opportunity for expanded media coverage. Flying fists were now witnessed by millions more people than had ever witnessed previous punch-ups during those dear departed days of the six-team era. Consequently, the league started to take some heat. So did the team.

"Our chemistry was right and how we played was right,

for the city," left-winger Bill Barber explained later. This was a new team in a town that was new to professional hockey. Fan support was crucial. Players wore their new orange and black uniforms with pride. "We were an aggressive team that pursued the puck hard and would do anything to win. That's what won the city over." So there.

"If we can, we'll intimidate our rivals," Philadelphia coach Fred Shero admitted freely. Ironic words from a somewhat cerebral former New York Ranger who was never particularly physical or aggressive himself. "That just wasn't my nature," Shero shrugged. Nevertheless, he continued, "I don't see it as dirty tactics. There are lots of ways to play this game. This is our way. It's a rough game. Our way works." By 1974, Shero's words were more than opinion. They were fact.

It was soon obvious that for the Flyers, "our way" meant much more than terrorism on ice. If it is true that perception becomes reality, then the Philadelphia Flyers' nickname was a deserved one. However, there was another reality, one that was to become as obvious as the first: the Flyers were not only a hard-fighting team, but also a hard-playing team of tremendous skill. It was this reality that propelled the relatively new expansion team to two consecutive Stanley Cup victories in a row. It was a reality that, for the next decade, more than matched whatever negative image the team might have had. This was a team of talent, enough to make Philadelphia the first expansion team to earn the coveted Holy Grail of Hockey.

Build an Arena ... And a Team, Too

The pressure had been mounting for years. At last it was going to happen. The

National Hockey League was going to get bigger. In fact, it was to double in size, growing from six teams to twelve. The official announcement came in 1965: immediately following the 1966–1967 season, the NHL's Board of Governors would accept proposals and hear presentations from parties interested in operating new league teams (20 years and many more expansions would pass before the term "franchise" would become fashionable). The interested parties had a mere two years to prepare their plans and pitches. There was no time to waste.

Getting the nod of approval from the NHL wouldn't be easy. It would take gathering together astute businessmen (with deep pockets) capable of underwriting a team's first, formative years. It would take a city of a certain size, one capable of delivering enough fans to fill a major arena for much of the season, certainly during semifinals and finals. And it would, of course, take the arena itself to hold all those fans — at least 12,500 of them.

First major problem: Philadelphia didn't have an arena of that size. In fact, there was just one facility in the whole city that had a permanent ice plant, and it was an old, rundown west-side arena with a seating capacity of just 6000. This meant the odds of Philly successfully fronting a new NHL team were long. (In this, Philadelphia was not alone. As strange as it seems today in our 32-team era, two other NHL hopefuls, Minneapolis-St. Paul and Los Angeles, did not have adequate arenas either.)

No arena? This didn't deter William Putnam. He saw Philadelphia's potential. He also possessed the experience to realize it. In 1964, the former banker had successfully managed the purchase of Philadelphia's NFL Eagles for Washington D.C.-based businessmen Jerry Wolman and Earl Foreman. Together with Wolman and Eagles' Vice-President Edward Snider, Putnam began putting a plan together.

Putnam was sure they had the right city. He and Foreman were confident they could raise the $2 million entry fee (a substantial sum in 1967). But before the visionaries could even think of building a team, they had to build a place for it to play. From the very outset, Washington, D.C. building contractor Jerry Schiff had been a member of Philadelphia's "pre-ice" team. Building plans were drawn up. Wolman agreed to finance the new showcase. On February 9, 1966, just a day after Putnam's team presented their proposal to the NHL, the governors announced that Philadelphia would become an NHL city.

That week, the whole of Philadelphia did a double-take. Residents of the city were stunned. For an entire year, Putnam's team had managed to work in virtual secrecy. Few knew that Philadelphia was even interested in making a bid for one of the expansion teams. "We tried to keep it quiet," Putnam confessed to the *Philadelphia Bulletin* the day the group made their presentation. "We were just afraid we might foul it up otherwise."

The secrecy gave the team-to-be an unexpected advantage. The bid and the NHL's decision was a sudden and very exciting surprise — just what was needed to galvanize the city. Spurred on by the success of the NHL go-getters, city hall released five acres of its land holdings for the soon-to-be constructed Broad Street sports complex that would be called the Spectrum. Very shrewdly, the owners announced a public contest to name the team. While Putnam's group may have owned the team, by allowing the public to choose its name, the newly christened Flyers really belonged to the people of Philadelphia. That was just the way the owners wanted it.

As the foundation of the Spectrum was laid, the foundation of a future Cup-winning team was being created through the 1967 expansion draft. Two of the team's goalies, Doug Favell and Bernie Parent, were among the first to put on new Flyers uniforms. Both netminders had led the Ontario Hockey Association's Niagara Falls Flyers to Canada's junior hockey Memorial Cup. For Parent, it was the first of many career milestones, most of which were earned while in a Flyers uniform.

"He was the best in the world at what he did," coach Fred Shero reminisced later. Parent was to prove the coach's assertion in many ways, including winning the "Triple Crown" of hockey: the Vezina Trophy as the league's best regular season goalie, the Conn Smythe Trophy as the Most Valuable Player in the playoffs, and the coveted Stanley Cup. It was a feat he achieved not once, but two years running.

It might not have happened at all. In the 1970–71 season, the Flyers — who had won just 3 of 15 playoff games — were desperate simply for a chance to play for the Cup. That meant changing the roster. In a complex three-way deal, Philadelphia traded Bernie Parent to Toronto for center Rick MacLeish, who was then skating for the Boston Bruins. "[MacLeish] is the kind of young player we must have to build a Stanley Cup contender," manager Keith Allen argued at the time, "and the only way we could get him was to move one of our goalies."

There were no hard feelings on Parent's part. "The Flyers had to make the deal to improve themselves for the future," he explained graciously. He could not have guessed that, three years later, it was *he* who would be the Flyers' biggest improvement for the future. Meanwhile, he would console himself by learning crucial netminding lessons from his boyhood idol, Leafs' legend Jacques Plante. The Flyers would benefit in ways none could imagine.

"Parent was absolutely indispensable to the team. Without him there would have been no Stanley Cups in Philadelphia." These words of praise were spoken by center Bobby Clarke. Not long after the star center joined the Flyers in 1969, he was earning many words of praise himself. Nothing — not injuries, pain, or fatigue — kept the somewhat diminutive, diabetic Clarke from giving the team everything he had. And he had plenty. Over the next few years, he was a veritable powerhouse. Through his enormous face-off skills and deadly passing ability, Clarke racked up three 100-point seasons while with Philadelphia, and broke Bobby Orr's three-year lock on the Hart Trophy, hailed as MVP in three of the next four years.

The Flyers welcomed other players in 1972, including Bill Barber. Drafted as a center, Barber was moved by the team's coach to left wing, to play alongside Clarke. Good move; in his rookie season, Barber scored 30 goals. Moreover, he quickly proved to be a defensive strength as well, and would more than earn his right to wear his Stanley Cup rings. Other future Stanley Cup stars were recruited, including wingers Ross Lonsberry and Bill Flett. Then, in 1973, in a move that redeemed him in the eyes of many, Keith Allen reacquired Bernie Parent.

The Fog Descends

Players weren't the only men rotating through the team's early years. Coaches came and went as well. In 1971, Fred Shero, a successful minor league coach who had led various teams to championships, was called upon to do the same for the frustrated Flyers. When he unpacked his bags as the team's third and newest coach, the Flyers had posted a so-so record of 96-135-73. Over the next seven seasons under his leadership, Shero's Heroes went 308-151-95. By the end of

1979, only Montreal and Boston achieved higher regular season standings for the decade.

How did Shero do it? Answers were less than definitive. Having good talent helped — it always does. However, it took a special man to mould the talent, and Fred Shero was special. It wasn't his fault if people had a difficult time explaining just how or why. Nicknamed "The Fog" by winger Gary Dornhoefer, absent-minded Shero was something of an enigma. He created a weird 16-point system for success, which he drilled into his players incessantly. Scotty Bowman took note, intent on cracking the code of this upstart team.

"Sometimes I see [Shero] and think he doesn't know what day it is," the Canadiens' coach said. "Other times, I'm sure he is a genius who has us all fooled." Something certainly had them fooled. Theories abounded. Could it be that a singer was the secret? The venerable Kate Smith's stirring rendition of "God Bless America" at the start of important home games did more than rattled the Spectrum rafters. It seemed to somehow inspire the Flyers to victory.

If Shero's methods were ahead of their time, his interaction with individual players was a little "out there" as well. "What's he like?" a reporter asked Larry Goodenough two years after the defenceman joined the team.

"I couldn't tell you," Goodenough stated flatly. "I've never met the man."

Players would discover little notes from Shero in their lockers, and they would read the words of wisdom he had chalked on the blackboard. Among his most famous: "Win together now and we walk together forever."

The winning really began in earnest during the 1972–73 season. With their opening-round playoff series with Minnesota tied two games apiece, a game-five score of 3-3 sent the teams into overtime — and Gary Dornhoefer into action. Eluding the Northstars' defence, he flipped in a desperate backhand shot that sent goalie Cesare Maniago sprawling and put the puck firmly against the net. The Flyers won the next game by a comfortable 4-1 score. On to round two, and the Canadiens. Off to a solid start, the Flyers won the first game at the Forum, but that was all. Nevertheless, as Dornhoefer said after his winning goal against the Northstars, "I think we've turned the corner and I want to be here when this team wins the Stanley Cup." He — and the city of Philadelphia — wouldn't have to wait much longer.

The First Expansion Dynasty
Canadiens star goalie Ken Dryden was absent in the 1973–74 season. Seriously Injured? Deathly ill? Ridiculously traded?

None of the above. How about "temporarily retired?" It was true. The man who some felt was most responsible for the Canadiens' rise to prominence in the early 1970s was taking time out to article with a Toronto law firm. It was a decision that would have a crucial impact on the Flyers' fortunes, and may have been one reason that Montreal was nudged out of East Division first place by Boston. The Bruins'

Esposito, Orr, Hodge, and Cashman took top positions in the league's scoring race. Two other decisions made by the Flyers themselves proved propitious.

The Flyers welcomed back Bernie Parent. Many fans did not — the goalie was booed when he first skated onto the ice — because the team traded Doug Favell back to the Leafs to reacquire Parent. Before the season was through, however, fans were cheering. The other decision: 24-year-old Bobby Clarke was made the youngest team captain in the NHL. Under his leadership, the Flyers placed first in the West Division with 112 points, beating out favoured Chicago. Then it was time for the playoffs.

The Rangers put Montreal away after six games. The Flyers beat Atlanta four straight and then faced New York. Parent's game-one shutout set the pace, but it took another six brutal games — and his unwavering netminding excellence — before the Flyers waved goodbye to the Rangers. Meanwhile Chicago ended the Los Angeles Kings' season in five games. In the East, Boston quickly dispatched Toronto, and then took a six-game series against Chicago. Suddenly, the league-leading Flyers and Bruins were the only teams left on Stanley Cup ice.

After seven seasons, the Flyers were Cup contenders. Oh, but what foes they faced! In the season just concluded, the Bruins had beaten or tied Philadelphia in 27 of their 28 games. Flyers fans must have shuddered.

The Cup series began and ended in a "Bobby" contest

between Orr and Clarke. In game one, Clarke tied the score 2-2 in the third period. Just before the clock put the teams into overtime, Orr managed to put one past Parent for the Bruins victory. Game two in the Boston Garden was 12 minutes into overtime when Clarke banged a rebound past Gilles Gilbert. The series was tied.

To the delight of delirious fans, Flyers won twice on home ice. Then, in Boston, the Bruins beat back the gloom and won game five handily, 5-1. Game six found the teams in Philly. Kate Smith sang, the fans screamed, and the Flyers scored. Rich MacLeish's first-period marker was still the only one on the scoreboard deep into the third. The Bruins pounded Parent, but the Flyers goalie was invincible. With less than two minutes to play, one Bobby (Orr) was penalized for holding the other (Clarke). When Orr skated off the ice, the game was really over before the buzzer sounded. One of the newest teams in the league had beaten one of the oldest.

For the very first time, the Cup belonged to an expansion team. More amazing still, this was the first Stanley Cup win for every single player in the Flyers' line-up. The next day, millions witnessed victory ceremonies at Independence Mall. The mayor spoke, the players spoke, and Kate Smith sang "God Bless America." She sang it again and again — six times in all.

The next season, the league welcomed two new clubs (Washington and Kansas City), and four new divisions were formed. The Flyers found themselves in the Clarence

Philadelphia Flyers: 1973–1975

Campbell Conference's Patrick Division. Final division standings — not points — would now determine playoff positions. Only one point behind the Bruins the season before, the Flyers did not really worry, and didn't need to. They finished the regular 1974–75 season with an incredible string of 12 victories in their final 14 games, tying for top spot with Buffalo and Montreal. "I don't think there was any doubt in our dressing room the following year about what was going to happen," Bill Barber later recalled. "We were going to win again."

When Toronto advanced to the quarterfinals, the Flyers were waiting. Four games later, the Leafs were history. It looked like it would go the same way with the New York Islanders — the Flyers won the first three games. Astonishingly, the Islanders fought back and won the next three (the team was used to it, having just recovered from a three-game playoff series deficit to beat Pittsburgh). Game seven was played inside the Spectrum. Kate Smith sang again, the fans screamed again, and once again, the Flyers scored. First it was Dornhoefer and then MacLeish, who scored a hat trick, securing a 4-1 victory and a spot in the finals. Now that the other new frontrunner, the Buffalo Sabres, had put the finish on Montreal's chances, people were calling it "The Expansion Series."

Parent was the hero of the first two games in the Spectrum, repeatedly denying the Sabres' front line any chances for victory. Bumper stickers read: "Only the Lord saves more than Parent." Final scores: 4-1 and 2-1, with

Bobby Clarke scoring the winning goal in game two. Buffalo won game three and four on home ice, but back in Philly, the Flyers clamped down hard and achieved a decisive 5-1 win. A change in goalie put Roger Crozier in the net for the Sabres. Like Parent, Crozier was superb, until Flyer Bob Kelly snuck one past the Sabres' netminder in the third. While Parent and the Philadelphia squad protected the lead, Bill Clement lengthened it by an insurance goal. The Flyers won the game 2-0 and took the Cup for the second year in a row.

The Broad Street Bullies could have "beat them up" for the Cup. However, while the team and the city celebrated, hockey pundits noted that there had only been two fights in the entire six-game series. That meant the Flyers had beat Buffalo with basic hockey skills — Shero's 16-point skills — instead of brawls.

More Playoffs and an Amazing Streak
Ken Dryden was back in net for Montreal in the 1975–76 season. Just to emphasize the fact, the Canadiens goalie snatched away the coveted Vezina Trophy that Bernie Parent had held two years running as Montreal finished the season in fine style, with 127 points. Parent's neck x-rays were back, too, and the news wasn't good. His injury would leave him out of the line-up for most of the season. Still, not many doubted that the Flyers could reach the Cup finals again. Could they win against the Canadiens? Could they win without Bernie Parent? True, Guy Lafleur had won the scoring race, but Bobby

Clarke was just six points behind. Another good omen: Flyers forward Reggie Leach scored 61 goals throughout the season. "I can release the puck as fast as anyone," Leach boasted. "Within 15-20 feet of the net, I'm deadly."

Not, however, as deadly against Dryden as his team-mates needed him to be. In the end, there was one good thing about the Flyers' third Stanley Cup series: it was mercifully short. Just four games was all it took for the Habs to take the cup back to Montreal. The deep strength of lines featuring the likes of Doug Jarvis, Jim Roberts, and Bob Gainey simply overwhelmed Philadelphia. After losing the first two games, Flyer Ross Lonsberry admitted, "They're so big you can't go through them and so strong you can't get around them."

The Flyers also found it tough to simply keep up with them. As Montreal left-winger Murray Wilson remembered later, "Our style was fast with smaller forwards. Our forte was speed." The Canadiens were goal-getters, too, with three markers from Steve Shutt, and a pair each from Jacques Lemaire and Guy Lafleur. Montreal left the usually high-flying Philadelphia team grounded.

Leave it to Habs goaltender Ken Dryden to provide a perspective on their Cup rivals. "People will see that we won in four straight games and think that it was easy," he explained during the dressing room celebration. "But they could not be more wrong. If you'll notice, we're drinking our champagne sitting down."

Dryden's take on the team was perceptive. The Flyers

simply refused to fold. In fact, after losing one of their first two games in the 1979–80 season, the Flyers would not lose a single game again for almost three months, creating an unbeaten streak of 25 wins and 10 ties.

This was a team that would simply not go quietly. In the 1980s, the Flyers fought for the Stanley Cup three more times (1980, 1985, and 1989). During that sensational period, the team finished first in its division nine times, second three times, and dropped to third place only twice. Philadelphia's remarkable achievements would be relived time and time again, as players such as Parent, Clarke, and Barber, as well as owner Ed Snyder, manager Keith Allen, and coach Fred Shero, were inducted into the Hockey Hall of Fame.

Chapter 5
Montreal Canadiens
Stanley Cup Victories: 1975–76, 1976–77, 1977–78, 1978–79

ho could imagine the playoffs without the Montreal Canadiens? Unthinkable. For the Habs and their fans, the playoffs were an annual ritual. More often than not, semifinals would almost certainly lead to the finals. In the last half of the 1960s, the finals had become an annual ritual, too. It was always the Habs against the whomever: Blackhawks, Red Wings, Maple Leafs, or St. Louis (twice). Chances were always good that the Canadiens would win the Stanley Cup, and they did so four out of those five years. However, at the start of the new decade, that predictable ritual came to an abrupt end.

In the 1969–70 season, personal problems and illness put stalwarts such as Jean Beliveau, Ted Harris, and Dick Duff

Jean Beliveau battles with Dave Balon of the Rangers
in a November 1968 game

(traded later in the season) in a deep slump. Goalie Gump Worsley was suspended without pay. Defenceman Serge Savard nursed a broken leg. By March, the team had slid to an almost unimaginable fifth place. As the season approached its end, the team rallied and managed fourth spot, tied with the New York Rangers. Then, the Rangers beat Detroit. Montreal's final game was against the Chicago Blackhawks.

Montreal Canadiens: 1975–1979

In the third period, Chicago led 5-2. Montreal was desperate to wrest enough scoring out of an already-lost match to put it in playoff position. It didn't happen. Worse, the coach's empty-net strategy in the final 10 minutes turned the 5-2 loss into an embarrassing 10-2 rout.

Not make the finals? Fans could live with that, painful as the notion was. But the significance of this final loss and the failure to simply score enough goals was much greater. For the first time in 22 years, mighty Montreal would not even make it to the playoffs! "It's like a bad dream," moaned Henri Richard. The *Montreal Gazette* featured a black-bordered headline: "R.I.P—A STANLEY CUP PLAY-OFF DYNASTY ENDS".

The end of the annual Cup-contender's streak may have really begun two years before, when revered coach Toe Blake finally called it a career. Even the new coach, Claude Ruel, well known for his work with the Canadiens' junior league (but with no major league experience), recognized he would work in Blake's shadow. "Me, I can only go down," the short, rotund French Canadian once admitted. "I can't go up." Ruel didn't mention the other direction that was open to him: *out*. At least, out of the coach's office. Unable to command the respect of his players, and marked with Cup defeat, Ruel went back to being a scout and then, later, assistant coach.

Perhaps General Manager Sam Pollock was thinking about the *Gazette*'s headline when he mused philosophically, "Remember, you've got to die to be born again."

Forging the New Team

Pollock brought in former defenceman Al MacNeil to take over as coach. The Quebec media was less than impressed. MacNeil didn't speak French. In coach Dick Irvin's day, language was less of an issue. Now it was the 1970s; separatism was in the air. Worse, there were bitter feuds between MacNeil and Henri Richard and John Ferguson.

By this time, a miracle had occurred: the Montreal Canadiens, third place underdogs, had reached the playoffs. Round one against the Boston Bruins, a classic seesaw series, is remembered by many Canadiens as a career highlight. Having won the first game, Boston was well on its way to winning the second, 5-1. Then Henri Richard scored, and the mantra became *let's get one more*. Captain Jean Beliveau got the tying goal. "One more" led to still others. Final score: 7-5, Habs. The Habs then bested the Minnesota Northstars in six and advanced to the finals.

Even there, feuding and fighting continued off the ice. MacNeil benched Richard in the fifth Cup game against Chicago. "How do you feel about that?" a reporter asked.

In spite of Richard's intention to say nothing, anger and frustration boiled over: "He's the worst coach I ever play for!" The feud, not the finals, became the talk of the town.

Nevertheless, the Habs beat the Blackhawks through the scoring prowess of Richard and new teammate Frank Mahovlich, and the extraordinary goaltending of Ken Dryden. A new farm-system arrival who started — and

One of the highlights of Jean Beliveau's career: Maurice Richard
congratulates Beliveau on wining the 1965 Stanley Cup
and the Conn Smythe Trophy

starred — in the playoffs, Dryden won the Conn Smythe
Trophy. Having helped make the Canadiens Stanley Cup
heroes again, Jean Beliveau exchanged his player's uniform
for a front-office suit and tie.

Despite the 1971 Cup victory, MacNeil, who had failed
to earn the respect of many of his players, was fired. Was he
bitter? Maybe, but as coach of a Canadien junior team once
again, at least he wouldn't have to put up with difficult star

players, a vitriolic French-Canadian press, and anonymous death threats.

Sam Pollock had his eye on someone he had known as a young coach in Ottawa's junior hockey league. More recently, Pollock had watched him work from across the ice, as the Canadiens fought for the Stanley Cup against the St. Louis Blues. He was a man worth watching, as he led a new expansion team to the finals three times. Not that this feat mattered much in the end. Somebody had to pay when a team loses the Cup series three times in a row. Or, when the owner's son is in charge. Like the new team in a Cup series, front-office politics proved to be a no-win situation, too. Scotty Bowman was fired. Sam Pollock probably couldn't help considering something else: Montreal-born Bowman spoke French. "Let's work together again," Pollock suggested. Bowman agreed.

Scotty Bowman's challenge in Montreal was much different than the one he had faced in St. Louis. It wasn't untried talent that he now had to shape and direct. Instead, he had to continually sharpen the skills of some of the finest players in the league to ensure that their performances were not dulled by complacency or arrogance. The new coach adopted a brilliant — but personally punishing — psychological strategy: he made himself the object of the team's enmity as he pried them out of comfortable over-confidence.

"The one thing we had in common," defenceman Larry Robinson later explained, "was that everybody hated Scotty."

The players had skill, they had speed, and now they had

hate. That was okay by Bowman. He didn't crave love. He craved results. And he wasn't above using the media to keep his team on their toes. A stunned defenceman would open the sports pages or turn on the radio and discover that he was going to be sitting out the next game or two. The "underperforming" player and his teammates would band together, challenge the decision, and the coach would then "reconsider." The relieved, determined player would then dash onto the ice and play like never before.

Some of the anger came from new players such as Steve Shutt, Guy Lafleur, and, later, Bob Gainey. The hardest thing about being a new Canadien, they all learned, was not that they might play badly. It was that they might not play at all. The wingers spent a lot of time on the bench. "My first couple of years with the Montreal Canadiens were among the most frustrating of my life," remembered Shutt. "I spent most of my time not even suited up." With so many great stars already on the ice, Bowman and Pollock could afford to wait for their newcomers to become even better than they already were.

Years later, Lafleur admitted, "they were not just thinking about the present, they were thinking about the future of the organization." But that was a mature perspective, which would come later. At the time, it was simply tough. Bowman had his own frustrations, too. It would take two years to get what he wanted. That first season — 1971–72 — was particularly trying: third place finish and out of the finals.

While Bowman didn't care about affection, Sam Pollock

didn't care about tradition. The general manager had no interest in preserving a "French-Canadian team," as his predecessor Frank Selke had. What Pollock cared about was having a *winning* team. Winners could be found in any ethnic or cultural community. You just had to look for them. Pollock found what he was looking for in the NHL entry draft. At the time, the system provided every team an equal opportunity to scout and draft the same players.

Pollock was a master draftsman. What was needed was careful planning and strategic thinking; one eye on players, but the other one on team standings (first place teams selected last; last place teams picked first). Pollock also knew how to make trades. One of the best, and possibly a deciding factor in winning the 1971 Cup, was obtaining Frank Mahovlich from ailing Detroit. Other new blood in the early 1970s: Ken Dryden in goal, Guy Lafleur and Mario Tremblay on right wing, Steve Shutt on left wing, and Larry "Big Bird" Robinson. Robinson, Serge Savard, and Guy Lapointe were the "Ministry of Defence."

With intuitive scouting and relentless prodding from the bench, Pollock and Bowman achieved what they cared about most. And how.

Cup After Cup

The objective was consistency — make the Stanley Cup a Montreal ritual again. Pollock and Bowman did it with the "Ministry of Defence," excellent goaltending, and four superb forward lines. Each line was responsible for making a distinct contribution:

#1: Goal-scoring — Steve Shutt, Guy Lafleur, Pete Mahovlich
#2: Two-way playing — Jacques Lemaire, Yvan Cournoyer, and Murray Wilson
#3: Checking — Doug Jarvis, Bob Gainey, and Jim Roberts
#4: Checking and scoring — Doug Risebrough, Mario Tremblay, and Yvon Lambert.

During the Pollock/Bowman era, the Canadiens accomplished stunning achievement after stunning achievement. In 1972–73, they had a mere 10 losses in the regular season, and capped that off with a Cup victory. From 1975–76 to 1978–79, the team dominated the league, winning the Stanley Cup each year. Only one other team has done this since. (New York Islanders, 1979-80 to 1982-83.). Indeed, in 10 seasons, the Habs played for the Stanley Cup six times — more than any other team — and won it every single time.

It happened like this: In the 1972–73 playoffs, it took the Canadiens six games to vanquish the tough Buffalo Sabres. Philadelphia then fell to Montreal in five games. The Canadiens would meet the Blackhawks in a series some called a battle of the goaltenders. More specifically, it would be between Ken Dryden and Tony Esposito.

In game one, Montreal walked over Chicago 8-3. Game two: Yvan Cournoyer contributed two goals to a 4-1 Montreal victory. Back in Chicago, the Blackhawks came back 7-4. Game four belonged to Dryden and the Canadiens: 3-0. In game five, neither Dryden nor his counterpart, Esposito, could see the puck, as Chicago won an 8-7 goal-a-thon. With a final score of 6-4, Canadiens took game six and the Stanley Cup, and playoff MVP Yvan Cournoyer carried off the Conn Smythe Trophy.

Then, for two long years, Canadiens watched the finals from the stands or in their living rooms. Philadelphia's Broad Street Bullies ruled. It wasn't just the Flyers' winning combination of punch-ups and scoring. Ken Dryden opted to article at a Montreal law firm. The fact that the Canadiens wouldn't equal the salaries paid by other clubs to their star netminders simply made his decision to leave that much easier. Guy Lafleur's slump was so deep that Bowman and Pollock considered trading him. Defenceman Jacques Laperriere sought retirement and, in 1975, so did the great Henri Richard.

Months before the 1975–76 finals, Philadelphia and Montreal fans caught a glimpse of what was to be. Gloves were on the ice between the two teams as early as a game in September, when Flyers captain Bobby Clark collided with the Habs' Doug Risebrough. The resulting melee cleared the benches.

"We won the Stanley Cup that night," Steve Shutt explained. "If you are going to beat the Stanley Cup champions, you have to beat them at their style because they dictate the game. Philadelphia was a tough team, so we had to prove that we were tougher."

To many fans, the finals battle between the Canadiens and the Flyers seemed inevitable. It seemed that way to the Canadiens, too. Ken Dryden (who had just returned to the team) recalled that even when they played other teams that season, it was the Broad Street Bullies they saw in their mind's eye. Bowman formulated new checking strategies designed to overwhelm front-liners such as Bobby Clarke, Bill Barber, and Reggie Leach. It was Leach who had scored 19 goals in 16 playoff games. Philadelphia had to be stopped. In the end, it took only four games.

In game two, Clarke, Barber, and Leach only got one shot apiece. Bowman's strategy was working. Meanwhile, the Montreal marksmen did their work, racking up the winning goals. The series tally: 4-3, 2-1, 3-2, 5-3. For Steve Shutt, the experience was especially sweet. When the final game was over, the one-time benchwarmer counted up 45 goals for the season. Even the Flyers' fans couldn't deny their admiration. Yvan Cournoyer and his team received a warm ovation as the captain skated around the Spectrum with the Stanley Cup held aloft. On the trip back to Montreal, Dryden handed out the lyrics to God Bless America — the Flyers' unofficial anthem — changing the lyrics to "God bless our Canada."

"We sang it all the way home," Dryden recalled.

The Canadiens' victory over the Broad Street Bullies was, in Serge Savard's words, "a victory for hockey. I hope that this era of intimidation and violence that is hurting our national sport is coming to an end."

Another year, another sweep. In 1977, after taking St. Louis in four, and the very competitive New York Islanders in six, Montreal readied itself to play Boston for the Cup. The Bruins anticipated the awesome power of the Canadiens before the finals, and tried to formulate a strategy: practising early, not practising at all, arriving at the arena early.

"We tried everything to beat them that first year," remembered Bruin Peter McNab. Thinking about the outcome, he added ruefully, "Maybe we shouldn't have shown up at all."

Jacques Lemaire scored three of Montreal's game-winning goals, including the overtime Cup winner. The series scoreboard read 7-3, 3-0, 4-2, and 2-1. Skating speed and skill on the Canadiens' part led to multiple awards. Lafleur won the Art Ross, Hart, and Conn Smythe (26 playoff points); Robinson took the Norris; Dryden won the Vezina, and Scotty Bowman took home the Jack Adams, for the league's best coach.

Montreal's performance throughout the next season, 1977–78, was simply phenomenal: 28 consecutive wins, number one position, and 16 points ahead of Boston. Nevertheless, there wasn't one Canadien who thought it was going to be as easy for the team to beat Don Cherry's Bruins in the finals this time around.

It certainly looked easy in game one, as the Habs registered a 4-1 victory. But the Bruins' goalie, Gerry Cheevers, made things tougher in game two. It took an overtime goal by

Guy Lafleur to secure the 3-2 win. At the start of game three, Cheevers received a standing ovation. He said thank you by shutting out Montreal 4-0. Game four's hero was Boston's Bobby Schmautz, who managed an overtime goal for a 4-3 victory. With the series tied 2-2, Larry Robinson led the scoring and Montreal won, 4-1. Bruins fans were on their feet as their team skated out into the Boston Garden for game six. The fans were on their feet again when Brad Park scored the game's first goal. That was their last reason to stand up. Montreal's Shutt, Tremblay, and Rejean Houle made it 4-1 and won a third consecutive Stanley Cup. Larry Robinson held a second cup — the Conn Smythe Trophy.

At the end of the 1978–79 season, Scotty Bowman must have been apoplectic. That old Hab problem had reared its ho-hum head again. "We'd become a little sloppy, a little complacent," Dryden admitted later, when recalling how the team lost to Detroit in the season's last game. That loss allowed the Islanders to become overall league leaders.

The Canadiens were losing game seven of the semifinal series to the Bruins, 4-3. Chances for a fourth Cup were slipping away when — no, it couldn't be! Don Cherry, caught with too many men on the ice? It was true, and on the resulting power play, Jacques Lemaire gave the puck to Guy Lafleur and, "without thinking," Lafleur recalled, "without even looking — I just let it go." It was a shot that the Bruins' goalie, Gilles Gilbert, couldn't stop. Then Yvon Lambert took a shot. Gilbert couldn't stop that one either.

"We were all laughing. That was all we could do," Canadien left winger Bob Gainey later recalled. "We looked at each other and we laughed and laughed. I don't know whether we were happy because we'd won or happy because we hadn't lost." On to the Stanley Cup finals!

Nobody in Montreal was laughing when the New York Rangers forged ahead in game one and Dryden was pulled in the third period. He was devastated. The Rangers took it, 4-1. Just before game two, goalie Michel Larocque was injured in a pre-game warm-up. Dryden was back in. Things started badly. The Rangers scored twice on their first two shots. But those were the only goals they scored in the game. All the other scoring was Montreal's. Final tally: 6-2. The Montreal squad was victorious again in game three, 4-1.

Twenty years later, Scotty Bowman was still watching tapes of game four, a performance as close to perfection as anyone could hope for. Bob Gainey didn't need tapes. The memory of the game — and winning the Conn Smythe Trophy — would be with him always. In that game, Gainey charged into the corner for the puck and collided with Ranger defenceman Dave Maloney. Both went flying; Maloney to the ice, Gainey towards the goal. He tied the game 3-3. Phil Esposito scored to send the Rangers ahead. Then Gainey scored again. In overtime, Serge Savard put the puck in again, making it a 4-3 win for Montreal.

Eighteen thousand fans were waiting for the Habs to take the sixth game at the Forum. New York's Carol Vadnais answered Rick Chartraw with a goal of his own, and then Jacques Lemaire and Bob Gainey answered with three goals in return. With the score sitting at 4-1 six minutes before the final siren, fans were already starting to celebrate, counting down the last 45 seconds. A few minutes later, they hoisted series hero Bob Gainey to their shoulders and carried him around the Forum in victory.

It had been a decade to remember, a decade based on skill, speed, and hate. By 1979, the skill and speed had never been better. And the other? By then, the hate had been replaced by respect, and the results were there for all to savour: six Stanley Cup victories, and admittance into the Hockey Hall of Fame for no less than nine of the men who had achieved them.

Chapter 6
Edmonton Oilers
Stanley Cup Victories: 1983–84, 1984–85, 1986–87, 1987–88, 1989–90

n the summer of 1971, a shockwave reverberated through the North American hockey world: the World Hockey Association was a reality. The WHA would give the game more fans, more revenue, and more profile than ever before. At first, the heart of the league was Western Canada, where the Winnipeg Jets, Alberta Oilers, and Calgary Cowboys drew the newly faithful. The upstart league gave its competitor, the NHL, a lot of headaches. The first migraine hit just a year after the league's formation, when NHL star Bobby Hull "defected" and signed with the Winnipeg Jets. Gordie Howe and others soon followed, bleeding the NHL of some of its best players. By the 1975–76 season, the new league boasted 14 teams.

Growing pains were severe. WHA franchises folded, foundering on the rocks of bankruptcy. By 1977, the Oilers — now called the Edmonton Oilers — were just one of eight clubs left. Among the teams that fell apart was the Indianapolis Racers. During their last season, a 17-year-old scoring sensation was on their roster. The Jets bid on the young rising star, but the Oilers upped the ante to $800,000. Wayne Gretzky packed his bags for his new home up in Canada.

The next season was to be the WHA's last. Four of its teams were merged into the NHL. Each was allowed to protect only four players from that last 1978–79 season. Among those teams was the Edmonton Oilers. Among its protected players, young Wayne Gretzky.

New Coach, New Vision
By 1981, during the Edmonton Oilers' second NHL season, coach Glen Sather had begun to implement brand new hockey concepts; concepts he had been thinking about for a long time. They had first caught his eye 10 years earlier, about the same time that the Alberta Oilers were a brand new team in that brand new league.

Sather hadn't experienced his hockey vision inside the rinks and arenas of Canada or the U.S. The future Oilers' coach had noticed it, instead, in Europe, as he'd watched midget hockey players battle it out in Finland and Sweden. What he saw might have been a tried and true style on the other side of the Atlantic, but it was brand new to the NHL: a hell-bent-for-leather offensive style based on speed. Sather knew that he needed to introduce more than the new style to the team. He would find players who were comfortable with that style; who knew how to work its magic. Through scout Barry Fraser, he would import fast-skating European stars.

The young man who was to become the team's — and perhaps the NHL's — most memorable player, Wayne Gretzky, was a product of home-grown Canadian minor hockey. One to watch, even at the tender age of 10, he was one Canadian player who had no trouble at all with Sather's offensive concept. He proved it in his first NHL season, scoring 51 goals, earning 137 points, and winning the first of nine Hart Trophies.

But Gretzky was human. He had a weakness and knew it: defence. Fine. Sather and Fraser would seek out newcomers who could compensate for that weakness. When he arrived from Finland in 1980, Jari Kurri hardly spoke a word of English. It didn't matter. He and Wayne Gretzky spoke fluent "hockey-ese" together. Kurri was the defensive forward that Gretzky — and Sather — needed.

Sather and Fraser looked other for players who could keep up with Gretzky and receive his passes, players such as center and left-winger Mark Messier. They looked for good defence and found Paul Coffey. They watched for a player who could protect the leads the Oilers generated, and slam the door on opposing teams. Someone like former WHA goalie Grant Fuhr.

And Gretzky? During 1981–82 season, he had earned himself a record-shattering 212 points. Something was working.

Cup Contenders Just Five Years In

Everything seemed to be coming together so quickly. By 1982, many fans were already starting to think "playoffs!" These were high expectations to have of a team this new. Were they realistic? There were thoughtful nods of assent. People remembered the St. Louis Blues. In their very first season, 14 years earlier, the Blues had not only managed a playoff berth, they'd put themselves into a Cup battle with the Montreal Canadiens. Of course, the Blues had lost, but they had, nevertheless, made the Habs sweat. St. Louis had been *this* close, and had liked the experience so much that they became Cup contenders the next two consecutive years.

So, it didn't necessarily take years to get to a playoff position, not if a team had what it took. And what it took was exactly what the Edmonton Oilers seemed to possess in abundance: a number of young, talented players, all on the same team, all coming into their prime at the same time, and a coach who knew what to do with what he had. "So what if the other team has a power play?" Sather told his players. "You get the puck and you go! Look for the scoring opportunity! Offence, offence, offence!" And the players would listen.

The team's rapidly growing prowess seemed to back up its promise. In 1981, there was a particularly stunning upset victory over the Canadiens. No playoff position, it's true, but a good omen nonetheless. One step forward, one step back: an embarrassing divisional semifinal loss to the L.A. Kings in 1982. No finals that year. (That left it up to the New York Islanders to sweep the Vancouver Canucks in four to take the Cup.)

Hopes ran high as the 1982–83 season began. By then it was obvious that most of the team's players — perhaps sensing there was greatness in the making — had made the decision to stick with Edmonton. They were a team off the ice, too, socializing amongst themselves in the tradition of the Montreal Canadiens. "Welcome to the team," they'd tell new draftees. It was more than lip-service. Second-year players would make the newcomers feel that welcome by taking them out for dinner.

Deep into the season, the team's performance increased. By the end of it all, they were ahead of the Islanders by a healthy 10 points. This could be the team, people thought, and this could be its year. The Oilers could be the first Western Canadian team to win the Stanley Cup since 1925 — the year the Victoria Cougars beat the Montreal Canadiens. When the semifinals were through, the five-year-old Edmonton Oilers faced the powerhouse New York Islanders (winner of three consecutive Stanley Cups) in the Stanley Cup finals.

Game one: a 2-0 shutout for a very feisty Islander goalie, bearded Billy Smith. There was his mug, on the front page of the *Edmonton Journal.* Headline: "Public Enemy No. 1." Game two: ouch! 6-3, Islanders. Smith, that netminding maniac, had Sather in a lather and the Oilers frustrated. If you can't control your emotions, you can't control the puck. Maybe this Cup business took more than youthful vitality and energy. Maybe it took experience, too. Game three: 5-1, Islanders. This was definitely not good. Game four, it was all over: Islanders 4, Oilers 2. The Islanders took the Cup. And the Oilers? Well, they would be back the next year, lessons learned — and remembered.

Revenge Is Sweet
The 1983–84 season was another terrific one for Gretzky, Messier, Kurri, Fuhr, and the rest of the Oilers. When semifinal time rolled around, it was a short flight down to Calgary. "You want a playoff chance?" taunted the Flames, "Work for it." Calgary wasn't going to be snuffed out by the Oilers the way it had been the previous year. Just to prove the point, the Flames stung the Oilers with a couple of overtime victories in what was a protracted, nasty, seven-game series. What really counts, though, is the number of games a team wins, not how the games are won. With a final, decisive, 7-4 victory, the Edmonton Oilers advanced to the Cup series.

Meanwhile, the New York Islanders were wondering, "Hey, think we can we make it five Cups in a row? It's been done: Montreal Canadiens, in the '50s." The Islanders had won an impressive 50 of 80 games, earning the team the Patrick Division title. New York was more than ready for another Cup Victory. *Why not?* Thing was, though, Edmonton had skated away at the end of the season with 57 victories, tops in the league.

The film projector whirred and the Oilers sat there in the flickering light, eyes glued to the screen. Horror films, really: Islander playoff victories, last year's humiliating four-game Cup series. Weren't the memories bad enough? No, not when you could profit by reliving the agony. The task: study the opposition. The objective: learn from past mistakes. It was time to take revenge.

In hockey, as in life, age provides experience, instilling wisdom and perspective. That's the upside. In hockey, as in life, age has a downside: physical limitations and pain. Going into the finals, there was plenty of pain in the New York dressing room. Mike Bossy came down with tonsillitis. Bryan Trottier taped up broken ribs. Bob Nystrom limped around with a bad knee. Dave Langevin and Stefan Persson? Each of them was wincing with the agony of a separated shoulder. Goalie Smith was suffering from a pulled groin muscle. By game three of the Cup series, leg cramps had driven Denis Potvin off the ice. *Pass the liniment. Hand me my crutch. Where are those darn pills?*

Islander Bill Torrey put it into perspective: "In five years we had one bad week. Unfortunately it came at the wrong time. The Oilers were very well prepared. They were fresh …" Yes, they were. The Oilers had just come off nine days of rest. But then, in a simple phrase, Torrey said something much more telling when he added, "… they were young." They had that and something else, too: experience. After that previous Cup series defeat, the Oilers were far more experienced than they had been the year before. It didn't take long for the rest of the world to recognize that youth plus experience equalled the Stanley Cup.

Glenn Anderson, who scored 50 goals that season, and who would eventually tally up 93 playoff goals throughout his stay with the Oilers, remembered the team's thinking. "All we wanted to do was walk out there with one win under our belts because we knew we were going back to Edmonton to play three games. We knew we could play well at home."

Oiler Kevin McClelland gave them that win, with a single third-period goal in game one. Then, goalie Grant Fuhr, who turned away 38 shots, and the impenetrable defensive squad, fought off five New York power plays. Glen Sather sent in a continuing stream of fresh power skaters to wear down the aging Islanders. Final score: 1-0. After 10 straight losses to the Islanders, it was a wonderful start to the series. New York roared back in game two, 6-1, while fans threw beer at the Oilers' bench and chanted M-I-C-K-E-Y M-O-U-S-E.

The Oilers were back in game three. The critical goal of the game came in the second period, with New York leading. Facing down two Islander defenders and still 30 feet from the crease, Mark Messier snapped a wrist shot past Billy Smith. Final score: 7-2. The loss forced New York coach Al Arbour to pull Smith out of the line-up, much to the raucous delight of Edmonton fans. The only good news for the losing Islanders? Grant Fuhr was injured and would not return for the duration of the series.

Game four was a scoreboard rerun: same numbers (7-2), same team, but this time, the first and last goals came from Gretzky, his first of the series. "We're happy we're leading 3-1, but that hockey team is a four-time champion," Gretzky commented cautiously after the win. "If we think we're in, we're in trouble. We haven't won anything, yet." He did his best to change that, contributing two goals in game five. It wasn't until the third period that New York made the scoreboard at all — too little, too late. Final score: 5-2. "It's a crushing defeat," admitted Islander Mike Bossy.

"Most of us are pretty young guys," a more confident Wayne Gretzky remarked after the final game. "Now that we've made the breakthrough, the best is yet to come."

A Dynasty in the Making

At the start of the 1984–85 season, the momentum was still there. The Oilers played 15 games straight without a loss. By the end of the season, they placed four points behind Philadelphia, and celebrated scoring champs Wayne Gretzky (73) and Jari Kurri (71). During the fast-paced playoffs, in which the team set 25 NHL records, they disposed of the L.A.

Kings, Winnipeg Jets, and Chicago Blackhawks to reach the finals and face the Philadelphia Flyers.

The first game, a 4-1 defeat in the Philadelphia Spectrum (in which Gretzky never even got a shot on goal) was a shocker for the Oilers. They bounced back to win game two, 3-1. Gretzky found himself and fired in three goals in the first 10 minutes of game three. Final score: 4-3. The Flyers fought back in game four and maintained a 3-1 lead until the Oilers scored another four straight goals. Philadelphia was awed again in game five as Gretzky set up the first two goals for Kurri and Coffey with a pair of behind-the-back passes. Messier scored another two on breakaways. There were four more goals by the game's end, and the Oilers celebrated an 8-3 victory — and another Stanley Cup.

Said a sombre Flyers defenceman, Brad Marsh, "They've got some of the greatest players in the world." But could the greatest keep on being great?

"If we're prepared to be dedicated enough and commit ourselves to the hard work that would be involved," Paul Coffey figured, "we could be a dynasty." The defenceman was right. It would just take a little longer than he or any of his teammates thought.

The 1986–86 season started well, and ended up going horribly wrong. The Oilers' chances at three consecutive Stanley Cups ended in the seventh game of the quarterfinals with the Calgary Flames. Rookie defenceman Steve Smith — celebrating his 21st birthday — banked an errant clearance off of Grant Fuhr's leg for an own goal, breaking a tie and ending the team's season prematurely.

But the next season, there were many reasons to celebrate: the Edmonton Oilers finished first in league standings, Gretzky won the scoring championship, Kurri finished second, and Messier was fourth. The team had earned a solid beat 12-2 playoff record. Then, it was time to meet the Broad Street Bullies in what would be the first seven-game Stanley Cup finals since 1971.

In Edmonton, the Oilers won the first two games of the 1987 Cup series, 4-2 and 3-2. The hard-fought contests won rookie Flyers goaltender Ron Hextall accolades from both sides. In game three, it looked like three in a row for the Oilers as they led 3-0 early in the second period. Flyers assistant coach, Paul Holmgren, began screaming at his team from the bench. As forward Rick Tocchet later recalled, "[Holmgren] yelled that we still had another thirty-eight minutes left and you don't roll over in the Stanley Cup playoffs." The team rallied and won, 5-3. It was a short reprieve.

The Oilers took game four handily by a score of 4-1. "Go Oilers, Go!" the *Edmonton Journal's* headline screamed as game five loomed. Eighteen hundred people were ready to scream, too, as they sat in front of a mammoth screen at the Edmonton Convention Centre. The crowd was quiet, though, as they filed out of the centre after the Oilers lost a 4-3 squeaker.

Before game six, rookie coach Mike Keenan carried the

Stanley Cup into the dressing room, hoping its presence would cast a winning spell over the team. Cup magic seemed to work, giving the Oilers two early goals. However, that new goaltender, Ron Hextall — whose standout performance would earn him the Conn Smythe Trophy — refused to allow the Oilers the additional goals they needed. The Flyers took the game, 3-2.

Back up in Edmonton, things got off to a rough start in the make-or-break game seven. Less than three minutes into the game, the Oilers were already a goal behind. Before the first period was over, however, Messier had tied the score. Kurri scored in the second period, and Anderson added one final goal in the third for a 3-1 Cup victory.

"The greatest high in my life is when I have that Stanley Cup in my hands and I raise it over my head," Wayne Gretzky said during the dressing room hysteria. Yet Gretzky proved magnanimous in victory. He held that Cup up briefly, then turned to Steve Smith (whose fumble had cost them the chance at the finals the year before) and handed it to him. This was Steve's moment, too.

The Oilers' playoff record the next year: 12 wins and two losses. The league's newest dynasty — you could call them that now — put away the Jets in five games, the Flames in four, and the Red Wings in five. The Edmonton Oilers would battle the Boston Bruins for the 1988 Stanley Cup. As great as the season was, the Oilers weren't quite the same team they had been. For the first time ever, the Oilers had placed second to the Calgary Flames. For the first time since 1981, Gretzky had not won the Art Ross as leading scorer. That honour had gone to Mario Lemieux. Little wonder: Gretzky had missed 16 season games after a stick-in-the-eye incident and a sprained knee. During the semifinals, defenceman Kevin Lowe played in a cast to protect a cracked left wrist and wore a flak jacket to shield cracked ribs.

The team was different in another way, too. After a two-month long contract dispute, Paul Coffey had been traded to Pittsburgh in November, and backup goalie Andy Moog had left for Boston, where fate would place him in front of his previous teammates a few months later in Cup action.

Gretzky's month-long absence due to the sprained knee wasn't all bad. Coming into the playoffs, he was more rested and fresher than he'd been in years. The big four — Gretzky, Messier, Kurri, and Anderson — had never been more formidable. They were ready to face the Big Bad Bruins for the Stanley Cup.

Played in Edmonton, the first two Cup games delighted the hometown fans, who watched the Oilers chalk up 2-1 and 4-2 victories. The Oilers captured a third win by a score of 6-3, with Gretzky setting up four of the six goals. Game four, played in the aged Boston Garden, was literally a steamy affair. The temperature rose to 28 degrees Celsius and the mist was so thick that the referee ordered the players to simply skate around the ice to disperse the fog. With the score tied 3-3 in the second period, play was suspended for good when a short circuit plunged the place into darkness. Fans evacuated the building relying on the feeble, faraway glow of the emergency lights. Both teams agreed to play game four once again in Edmonton. It was a goaltending match-up between former Oiler goalie Andy Moog and Grant Fuhr. Moog was great. Fuhr was greater. With a final score of 6-3, the Stanley Cup was hoisted aloft by the victorious Edmonton Oilers for the second consecutive time, and the fourth time in five years.

The Stanley Cup victory wasn't all Wayne Gretzky had to celebrate. In mid-July, there were wedding bells. Talking to his usher, Paul Coffey, on the big day, Gretzky shared an unsettling secret. Oilers owner Peter Pocklington was attempting to trade him. A week later, Bruce McNall, owner of the L.A. Kings, placed a phone call to Pocklington.

One More Time

The hockey club wasn't the only business Peter Pocklington owned — far from it. However, during the financially troubled early 1980s, owning a number of businesses often meant that the exposure to risk and ruin was greater. Times had been tough for the Oilers owner, and Gretzky was a great chip. It was time to cash it in. In August 1988, Pocklington sold the star he had purchased for $850,000 for $15 million. Edmontonians were first shocked, then outraged, and finally, saddened and depressed.

When the 1989 playoffs began, for the first time in

15 years there was no overwhelming favourite. There would be no Cup victory for the seventh place Oilers. The Calgary Flames saw their chance, beat the Kings (yes, Gretzky lost his chance at the Cup, too), advanced to the finals against the Canadiens, and defeated the Habs in six.

At the start of the new decade, the Oilers battled the Jets in the first-round playoffs. It wasn't easy — the Oilers were down 3-1 in the series before they sent their rivals limping back to the 'peg.

"Hi Wayne, how ya doin'?" the cocky Oilers then seemed to ask Gretzky and the L.A. squad.

The answer came quickly: "Not too good."

Certainly not good enough to advance to the finals. The Oilers trounced the Kings in four games. Then Edmonton packed up for Chicago to beat the Blackhawks in six games. In Boston, it was Cup time again — and a great time for Mark Messier.

Mark "Moose" Messier had been a linchpin on the team for years, winning the Conn Smythe Trophy as the team won its first Stanley Cup. Messier had tasted team leadership as interim captain when the Great One had sat out a month of his last season with a sprained knee. Now, recognition and responsibility were official. So long a leader in temperament and talent, Messier had earned the title to go along with it.

In the finals, captain Messier inspired the likes of Kevin Lowe, Randy Gregg, and Charlie Huddy to provide the stiff defence, and goalie (and Conn Smythe winner) Bill Ranford to keep opposition scoring low (the best the Bruins managed was two goals in three of five games). Messier was there to help set up the dazzling Cup-winning goals of Jari Kurri and "Kamikaze" Glenn Anderson in the four games — 3-2, 7-2, 5-1, and 4-1 that won the team its fifth cup in seven years. One other Oiler player who was recognized for his role in delivering that last, great Stanley Cup Victory, although he didn't even play in the series and no longer wore the white-and-blue Oilers uniform, was Wayne Gretzky. "Part of this Stanley Cup is his," acknowledged a grateful Gene Sather. "He got these players and this organization to where it is."

Chapter 7
Detroit Red Wings
Stanley Cup Victories: 1996–97, 1997–98

t was obvious that if Mike Ilitch believed in something strong enough, he would shrug off doubts and carry on, confident in his long-term vision. He was confident enough in 1959 to ignore people who said pizza pies were a fad. The bar owner he propositioned to allow him to install a pizza oven (to provide patrons a menu alternative) had nothing to lose. Two years later, there was enough cash and momentum to open a second location. After that, the name — Ilitch's name — Little Ceasar's Pizza was popping up all over.

Pizza wasn't the only thing curly-haired Mike Ilitch loved. He loved hockey. And in his neck of the woods, hockey meant the Detroit Red Wings. He loved them in the 1940s when he was a kid. He loved them in the 1960s when he was a younger man. He even loved them in the 1970s, when they were laid so low by bad trading decisions that they figured into the playoffs only twice in over 15 years. But Ilitch — like all ardent fans — was a true believer.

By the early 1980s, Ilitch owned one of the world's largest food franchises. In 1982, he bought himself another franchise. He became the proud owner of the Detroit Red Wings. Asking price: $13 million. The final price, as they say, was right: a mere $9 million. Many saw the purchase as something of a lifeline for a sinking squad. Ilitch preferred another metaphor. "It's a sleeping giant," he said.

Finding the Right Ingredients
In his early pepperoni-and-mushroom days, Mike Ilitch knew in his heart that his pizza business would thrive. He would simply make his pizzas better than the others. Was hockey any different? What he needed, once again, were the right ingredients.

Ilitch's first move was to hire a new general manager, Jimmy Devellano. Together, the two men then set about cooking up a new team. The quickest way to do that, it seemed, was to buy the talent they needed.

"We put a lot of thought and planning into our signings," said Devellano a couple of years later. Yes, and dollars, too. Ilitch spent millions more on players than other teams did. He spent a million alone (so people said) for one single player: Warren Young. The offers increased for prospects such as Adam Oaks ($1.1 million) and Ray Staszak ($1.3 million).

Criticism from other bottom-line-sensitive club managers grew. That didn't bother Ilitch and Devellano much. Lack of results did, though. They were buying, all right, but where was the talent they were paying for? Staszak played four games, scored no goals, and got one assist. Many of the newly acquired players had no more success elsewhere. Warren Young scored 22 goals in his debut season with Detroit, then returned to Pittsburgh. After 57 games, he had put the puck in the net a grand total of 8 times.

But Ilitch and Devellano didn't have to complain about one new player. The best of the large number of young players lured to Detroit was also one of the first: center Steve Yzerman. Selected in the 1983 entry draft, the Cranbrook, BC-born Stevie Y earned himself 87 points and his new team a very respectable third-place playoff-qualifying position at the end of the season. The Red Wings played extremely well in the semifinals against the St. Louis Blues (even the Blues' coach, Jacques Demers, admitted as much), but couldn't get past St. Louis goalie Mike Liut. Their season was over after four first-round games.

In spite of — or maybe because of — a fresh summertime infusion of college stars, Detroit remained stalled in third position in the 1984–85 season, but this did offer the team another chance at the playoffs. That was the good news. The bad news was that Detroit was eliminated by Chicago.

There was worse news still to come. A few months later, Detroit's star center was sidelined 29 games with a cracked collarbone. The Red Wings posted a shocking last-place 17-57-6 record, making the 1985–86 season its worst ever. And that was saying something; at that point, the club's history already stretched back over half a century.

"Not in my wildest nightmares would I have thought anything like this would happen," Jimmy Devellano told the *Hockey News*. The owner and his general manager hadn't found the right recipe for that "Stanley Cup Special" yet. Maybe they never would.

For the rest of the decade, the Red Wings might as well have installed a revolving door in the coach's office. Coach Harry Neale was history after 35 games of that disastrous 1985–86 season. The door revolved again and Brad Park walked in. The door was moving again just four months later, and Park was gone. Jacques Demers, the 17th coach in 18 years, then took up the hard-luck mantle. Demers was late of the Quebec Nordiques and the St. Louis Blues. His addition to the Red Wings seemed to be a very good move. The next season, 1986–87, Detroit placed second in its division and won four straight in the playoffs against the Blackhawks, thanks, in no small measure, to the standout performance of goalie Glen Hanlon. But the Edmonton Oilers killed whatever hopes Detroit had for going all the way. Still, they had come a huge distance in one season, from bottom of the heap to within four teams of being King of the Hill.

In 1988–89, Detroit reached first place in the division, but once again couldn't make the finals. Ironically, Steve Yzerman enjoyed his best year to date, firing in 65 goals and earning 155 points. In 1989–90, it was downhill all the way. The irony continued: Yzerman was third in scoring with 62 goals and 137 points. Nevertheless, the Red Wings finished last again. It was reason enough for Mike Ilitch to show Demers the (revolving) door. Bryan Murray then took on dual responsibilities of both coach and general manager. Devellano was still there, but had a new title on his business card: senior vice-president.

Stevie Y could only wonder if and when the turnaround would ever happen. Looking back on his own personal record of the decade, he had to be pleased; he'd had three consecutive 100+ point seasons (and three more were to follow). But one man — no matter how good he is — is not a team unto himself. Many others were needed.

That summer, during the Goodwill Games in Seattle, a Russian player slipped away from teammates. A few days later, Sergei Fedorov was a Red Wing. There were other new names on the roster. One was Mike Vernon. The team needed a goalie who had an excellent playoff history. Vernon qualified. In 1989, he had helped send the Calgary Flames to Montreal to win the Stanley Cup against the Habs in their own hallowed Forum.

A New Decade and a New Era

In the 1990–91 season, Detroit hung tenaciously to third spot and fought the good playoff fight in a seven-game cliffhanger with the St. Louis Blues. Then, the Red Wings fell off the cliff. The next year, things got better. The team's performance made them number one in their division, and number two in the league. They won over Minnesota in the first round of playoffs, but were beaten in four in the second, against the Chicago Blackhawks. In 1992–93, the Red Wings placed second in the division, fifth in the league. Finally, in 1994, the Western Conference champs endured the ultimate embarrassment, defeat in the finals against the San Jose Sharks, a team that had won a mere 11 games the year before. The coach's office door revolved again.

Mike Ilitch, didn't need to do any research on the man who was destined to walk into the coach's office next. Even as a hockey fan, Ilitch understood the significance of Scotty Bowman's many moves over the previous 20 years: St. Louis, Montreal, Buffalo, and, more recently, Pittsburgh. What did all these clubs have in common? Playoffs, finals, and Stanley Cups — lots and lots of Stanley Cups. In a sport with so many variables, Bowman was the one common thread of success woven through each of those teams' recent histories.

By the time Bowman arrived, Ilitch was already unlocking the team's Stanley Cup future by signing the first in a series of players that all spoke the same foreign language: Russian. First came Fedorov, and then, in 1991–92, Fedorov's friend and former captain of the Red Army team, Vladimir Konstantinov. By this time, Russian-speaking NHL players were no longer unique. Teams such as Calgary, Vancouver, and New Jersey had led the way. But while signing Russians wasn't new, coaches still had to figure out what to do with these players once they had them.

Scotty Bowman watched the Russians — new immigrants who barely spoke English — and saw how they played together, and how they quite naturally stayed together once off the ice. Bowman thought they would perform even better if they played as a unit. He correctly anticipated that their unity would help Detroit overwhelm other, defensive-minded, teams. First, however, there had to be enough of them to actually make the unit.

Bowman acquired Vyacheslav Kozlov, and then defenceman Viacheslav Fetisov. "Mistake!" critics jeered. But Bowman thought otherwise, observing that Fetisov was actually three players in one: superb defenceman, as well as someone who would act as assistant coach to young players, and be the cultural hero the Russians needed as "strangers in a strange land."

In the 1993–94 season, Fedorov played so brilliantly that he won both the Hart and Selke Trophies. It was a tantalizing taste of things to come. Bowman chose one more Russian: Igor Larionov. Now he had a powerful five-man unit. The proof? The team won the first six games Igor played. Then, after one single loss, the Red Wings won another nine in a row. In less than five years, Detroit had been transformed into "Russia on the Lake."

Obtaining the right players obviously was not enough. They had to play the right way. Bowman devised a new tactic, a system he called the "left-wing lock." When the opposition had the puck, Detroit players would attempt to contain the other team in a small area by quickly outnumbering them, forcing a bad pass. Bowman had dubbed it "left wing" because that was his preferred side where Detroit would force the play.

The 1994–95 season was shortened by labour problems. It worked to Detroit's advantage. After 48 games, they became regular-season champs, capturing the President's Trophy.

It had been a long, 29-year wait for the finals, but it was finally the Red Wings turn. For Scotty Bowman, it must have seemed like old times. But it turned out to be a pathetic anti-climax. The New Jersey Devils whipped Detroit four straight. With the exception of game one (2-1), none of the other games was even close.

In the 1995–96 regular season, the Red Wings outdid themselves and set an NHL record of 62 victories. Bowman worked them hard, perhaps to better his 60-game record with Montreal. However, when it came time to translate that power and authority in the playoffs, the team had little momentum left. Instead, the momentum belonged to the Colorado Avalanche, which rolled over Detroit in the semifinals. As they rolled, a sixth-game incident left the Red Wings particularly angry. Hardened veteran Claude Lemieux cross-checked young Detroit center Kris Draper from behind. There, right in front of the Red Wing bench, Draper's face hit the board so hard his jaw and cheek were smashed. The team couldn't retaliate and risk a penalty; they lost the game (and their chance at the finals) 4-1. It took plastic surgery and weeks of recuperation before Draper would look good — and play well — again. The Avalanche then went on to win the Stanley Cup in four against the Florida Panthers. The Draper incident helped galvanize this collection of players even further into a team. There would come a time …

Until then, Detroit would have to wait a little bit longer for its Stanley Cup celebration. No big deal; it had already waited over 40 years. The Red Wings had the right players (Stevie Y was celebrating his 500th goal), the right coach, and now all they needed was the right timing.

The Cup Years
Revenge was sweet at the end of the 1996–97 season. After beating St. Louis in six (against Grant Fuhr, no less) and Anaheim in a close four-game series, Detroit faced the Stanley Cup champions, the Colorado Avalanche. Call it Draper retribution time. Call it hard, controlled, goal-scoring hockey. Call it whatever you like, the Red Wings took Colorado, four games to two.

In game six, Fedorov left the ice with an injury. A few minutes later, Fetisov, the unofficial Russian assistant-coach, dashed into the dressing room. Was Sergei seriously hurt? The masseur shook his head. Loud, rapid-fire Russian between the two players filled the air. The masseur watched as Fedorov struggled up from the table and returned to the ice with Fetisov. Minutes later, Fedorov received a picture-perfect pass from another of the Russian unit, Kozlov, and scored the game-winning goal. It won the series, too. Detroit would meet Philadelphia in the finals.

A pair of newcomers had helped get the team to the playoffs, goalie Chris Osgood and aggressive forward Joey Kocur. However, it was Mike Vernon in the crease for post-season action, performing so brilliantly he earned himself the Conn Smythe Trophy as playoff MVP.

Against giant center Eric Lindros and the Philadelphia Flyers, the Red Wings still looked like underdogs. However, Scotty Bowman saw their weaknesses, and liked what he saw; some very slow skating and some very doubtful goalkeeping by Ron Hextall. He shared his perceptions with his do-or-die crew.

Detroit started strongly with a pair of 4-2 series-opening victories in Philadelphia. In the minutes before that first face-off in game three, the fans in Detroit's Joe Louis Arena were almost delirious with excitement. They were then rewarded with another, even more decisive, victory as center Fedorov scored twice and Detroit swept Philadelphia 6-1.

In game four, midway through the third period, with the score tied 1-1, Red Wing Darren McCarty rushed all the way down the ice, nimbly eluding Flyers defenceman Janne Niinimaa and firing past Ron Hextall to give Detroit the game-winning, series winning, Stanley Cup winning goal. The moment belonged to McCarty, but the Cup belonged to the team — Yzerman, Fedorov, Conn Smythe-winner Vernon, and all the others. Scotty Bowman couldn't resist: he laced up his skates and, as he had seen so many of his stars do in years past, skated the victory lap around Joe Louis Arena, the Cup held high. It had been a long, hard journey.

"What I've learned," said a weary but elated Yzerman, "is that there is the Stanley Cup winner and then there's everyone else. We've *been* everyone else."

Later, before an estimated one million fans in downtown Detroit, Vladimir — Vlad the Impaler — Konstantinov held the Cup high and announced, "This Cup is for you, for Detroit, for Michigan!"

Then suddenly came tragedy. Vladimir Konstantinov, Viacheslav Fetisov, and the team's masseur were near death after the limousine in which they were riding to goalie Chris Osgood's party careened out of control, roaring across the highway and smashing into a tree. Fetisov was most fortunate — his forward motion was checked by the mini-bar. But Konstantinov and the masseur were propelled against the hard partition. They both lapsed into weeks-long comas. Konstantinov's career ended; he has never fully recovered.

Few gave Detroit much of a chance for a Stanley Cup encore. The Flyers and the Devils were the favourites.

Detroit's post-Stanley Cup season wasn't one of its best. It got off to a difficult start when Sergei Fedorov did not sign his contract. It wasn't just the money. "Things would be different around here if my name was Sam Jones," he said bitterly, citing the differing standards of conduct (and perhaps comradeship) between the Russians and their North American teammates.

"Trade me," he told general manager Ken Holland, as he joined the Russian Olympic team. The Carolina Hurricanes made an offer of $38 million over six years. Would the Red Wings match it? They did, but he would have to work for it. He would get an additional $12 million if the Red Wings made the conference finals. Fedorov returned to Detroit, working hard to make amends with both North American and Russian teammates. In the end, he didn't have to wait six years for the money. He received it all in six months.

It wasn't easy. The long, dark shadow of the 1980s loomed large and the Red Wings finished in third place — good enough for a chance in the playoffs. If he was concerned about his team's chances, Bowman didn't show it particularly. All too often he had seen teams exhaust themselves in the regular season and have nothing left for the playoffs. He might have been thinking of that 62-game record that cost the team so dearly two seasons earlier.

Detroit battled with a trio of six-game series against Phoenix, St. Louis, and Dallas. As usual, the odds were against the Red Wings. Excitement in Motor City grew as the playoffs progressed. Detroit bettered Phoenix by four games to two. In spite of the odds, the Red Wings emerged victorious in the second round, winning four out of six against St. Louis. There was a collective sigh of relief — followed by a rousing cheer — as Detroit did it again, in the final round against Dallas. For the second consecutive season, the Detroit Red Wings proceeded to the Stanley Cup finals. Meanwhile, the Washington Capitals emerged from their own playoff battles as Detroit's 1998 series opponent.

The toughest component of the Capitals' finals line-up was goalie Olaf Kolzig ("Ollie the Goalie"). As outstanding as he proved to be, he couldn't compensate for the Capitals' failure to reverse the Red Wings' momentum in the Washington end. There was a strength, too, in the Detroit zone. Chris Osgood was outstanding in the net for the Red Wings. Detroit swept the series in four games: 2-1, 5-4, 2-1, and 4-1.

For coach Scotty Bowman, this was a milestone: eight Stanley Cup victories, equalling the record of that other coaching legend, Toe Blake of the Montreal Canadiens. Steve Yzerman, who had been the runner-up for playoff MVP trophy for his standout performance in the previous Stanley Cup series, reached a career milestone as well. This was the year the Detroit captain would hold high two of hockey's most sought-after prizes. His six playoff goals and superb support earned him the Conn Smythe. However, there would be no victory lap for Steve Yzerman, and he wouldn't have wanted it any other way.

The on-ice celebration of that second momentous Cup victory climaxed when a Detroit player who hadn't been able to suit up for the series was there to share the victory. Wheelchair-bound Vladimir Konstantinov was on the ice with his teammates. Yzerman turned and placed Lord Stanley's coveted trophy in his lap, and with fellow Russians Larionov and Fetisov pushing the chair, it was Vlad who made the victory lap around the Joe Louis arena.

"Not often," said Brendan Shanahan, "does a moment in hockey transcend sports."

Bibliography

Cole, Stephen. *The Last Harrah.* Toronto: Penguin Books, 1995.

Diamond, Dan, ed. *Years of Glory: The National Hockey League's Official Book of the Six-Team Era, 1942–1967.* Toronto: McLelland & Stewart Inc., 1994.

Diamond, Dan, ed. *Total Stanley Cup.* Toronto: Total Sports Canada, 2000.

Duhatschek, Eric, ed. *Hockey Chronicles: An Insider History of National Hockey League Teams.* Toronto: Key Porter Books, 2000.

Falla, Jack, ed. *Quest For The Cup.* Toronto: Key Porter, 2001.

Fischler, Stan. *Golden Ice: the Greatest Teams in Hockey History.* Scarborough, ON: McGraw-Hill Ryerson Limited, 1990.

Fischler, Stan. *The Rivalry, Canadiens vs Leafs.* Whitby, ON: McGraw-Hill Ryerson Limited, 1990.

Houston, William. *Inside Maple Leaf Gardens: The Rise and Fall of the Toronto Maple Leafs.* Toronto, Ont. McGraw-Hill Ryerson Limited, 1989

Bibliography

Hunter, Douglas. *Champions: The Illustrated History of Hockey's Greatest Dynasties.* Toronto: The Penguin Group, Penguin Books Canada Ltd., 1997.

Irvin, Dick, *The Habs: An Oral History of the Montreal Canadiens, 1940-1980.* Toronto: McLelland & Stewart Inc., 1991.

Jenish, Darcy. *The Stanley Cup: One Hundred Years Of Hockey At Its Best.* Toronto: McLelland & Stewart Inc., 1992.

McDonell, Chris, ed. *The Game I'll Never Forget.* Toronto: Firefly Books, 2002.

McFarlane, Brian. *Stanley Cup Fever.* Toronto: Stoddart, 1992.

McFarlane, Brian. *The Red Wings.* Toronto: Stoddart, 1998.

Pincus, Arthur. *The Official Illustrated NHL History.* North Vancouver: Whitecap Books, Ltd., 1999.

Podnieks, Andrew. *Hockey's Greatest Teams.* Toronto: The Penguin Group, Penguin Books Canada Ltd., 2000.

Strachan, Al, ed. *One Hundred Years of Hockey.* Toronto: Key Porter Books, 1999.

Weir, Glenn. *Ultimate Hockey.* Toronto: Stoddart, 1999.

Acknowledgments

With the possible exception of major league baseball, no other sport has been written about so passionately and voluminously than that of hockey. The thirst for narratives recounting the players, victories, and dramas of the National Hockey League is insatiable. I wish to thank and acknowledge all those authors whose works helped make this book possible.

Ultimate Hockey, by "self-confessed sports history addicts" Jeff Chapman and Glenn and Travis Weir proved indispensable. Also extremely helpful were Stan Fischler's *Golden Ice*, Dick Irvin's *The Habs*, and Darcy Jenish's *The Stanley Cup*. A special thanks to Stephen Cole, author of *The Last Harrah*. Neither an historian nor a hockey journalist or broadcaster, Mr. Cole, a freelance writer, is a fan's fan. His detailed, poignant, and, at times, hilarious recounting of the Leafs-Canadiens Centennial Year Stanley Cup series made my research a special pleasure.

About the Author

BC-born author Rich Mole has enjoyed an eclectic communications career, as a former broadcaster, a freelance journalist, and, for 20 years, the president of a successful Vancouver Island advertising agency. A lifelong fascination with history has fuelled his desire to write about the times and people of Canada's past. Rich now makes his home in Calgary, Alberta.

Photo Credits

All photographs are by Bruce Bennett Studios.

AMAZING STORIES

NOW AVAILABLE!

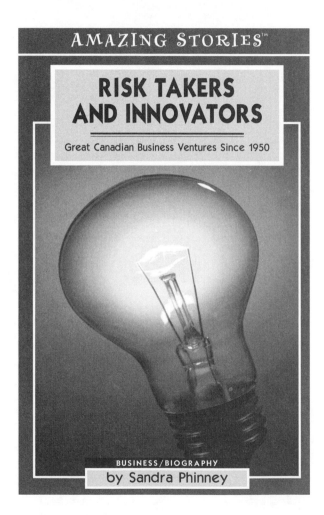

AMAZING STORIES™

RISK TAKERS
AND INNOVATORS

Great Canadian Business Ventures Since 1950

BUSINESS/BIOGRAPHY
by Sandra Phinney

Risk Takers and Innovators
ISBN 1-55153-974-8

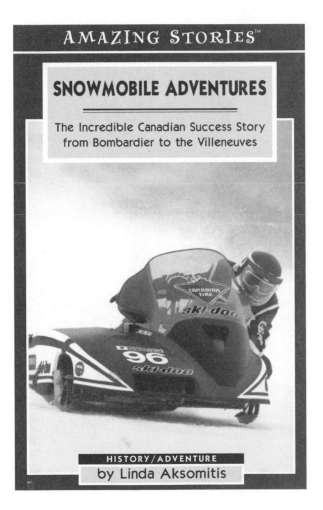

Snowmobile Adventures
ISBN 1-55153-954-3

Unsung Heroes of the Royal Canadian Air Force
ISBN 1-55153-765-5

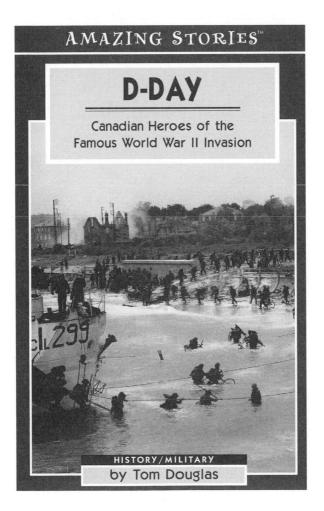

D-Day
ISBN 1-55153-795-8

AMAZING STORIES™

TRAILBLAZING SPORTS HEROES

Exceptional Personalities and Outstanding
Achievements in Canadian Sport

HISTORY/SPORT

by Joan Dixon

Trailblazing Sports Heroes
ISBN 1-55153-976-4

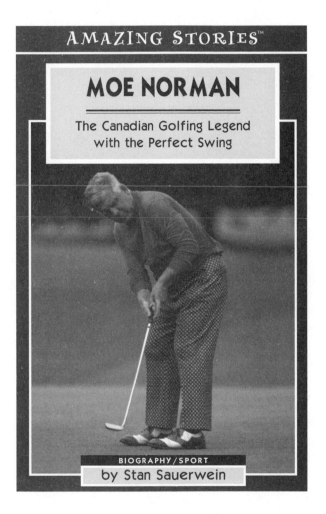

AMAZING STORIES™

MOE NORMAN

The Canadian Golfing Legend
with the Perfect Swing

BIOGRAPHY/SPORT

by Stan Sauerwein

Moe Norman
ISBN 1-55153-953-5

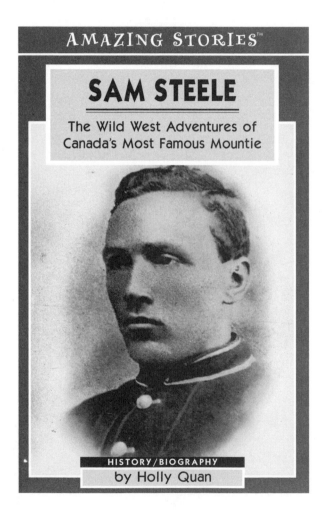

AMAZING STORIES™

SAM STEELE

The Wild West Adventures of
Canada's Most Famous Mountie

HISTORY/BIOGRAPHY
by Holly Quan

Sam Steele
ISBN 1-55153-997-7

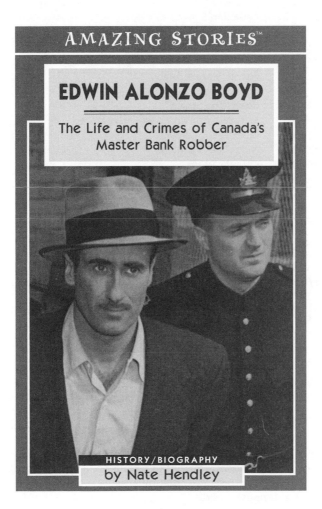

AMAZING STORIES™

EDWIN ALONZO BOYD

The Life and Crimes of Canada's
Master Bank Robber

HISTORY/BIOGRAPHY
by Nate Hendley

Edwin Alonzo Boyd
ISBN 1-55153-968-3

SELECTED OTHER AMAZING STORIES

These titles are available wherever you buy books. If you have trouble finding the book you want, call the Altitude order desk at 1-800-957-6888, e-mail your request to: orderdesk@altitudepublishing.com or visit our Web site at www.amazingstories.ca

New AMAZING STORIES titles are published every month. If you would like more information, e-mail your name and mailing address to: amazingstories@altitudepublishing.com.